IF I
DIE...

Please pray for
persecuted Christians?

— *[signature]*

IF I DIE...

RISKING DEATH TO LIVE FOR JESUS

VERNON BREWER

FOREWORD BY NOEL BREWER YEATTS

PUBLISHED BY WORLD HELP, INC. FOREST, VIRGINIA

If I Die...
Risking Death to Live for Jesus

By Vernon Brewer

Cover and interior art by Roark Creative, www.roarkcreative.com
Edited by Sheryl Martin Hash, Carmen McCauley

Copyright 2021 World Help
Printed in the United States of America.

ISBN# 978-0-692-16758-8

World Help
1148 Corporate Park Drive
Forest, VA 24551
worldhelp.net

World Help is a Christian humanitarian organization serving the physical and spiritual needs of people in impoverished communities around the world.

DEDICATION

Dedicated to thousands of Christ-followers
around the world who pay the ultimate price
for their faith.

CONTENTS

FOREWORD

I didn't know. I thought every little girl had a dad who traveled the world bringing back gifts like zebra-tail bracelets, Russian matryoshka dolls, and Hard Rock Cafe T-shirts from every corner of the globe. Didn't other dads come home with heroic stories of smuggling Bibles into China, being detained in Cuba, and followed by the police in Eastern Europe?

To me, my dad was part Jacque Cousteau, part Jim Elliot and just a little Indiana Jones. But it wasn't until I was older that I realized how important and needed his work really was.

Those early stories he told shaped me in ways I can never repay. My dad didn't just tell me how to live, he showed me and took me along for the ride. And his continued passion and work around the world, especially in the persecuted church, became the cornerstone of World Help and an integral part of our mission of help and hope.

As I now lead the organization he began, I am keenly aware of what has come before. Countless sacrifices have been made and so many lives have been lost by those willing to die for their faith.

But these are not just stories from the past. Unfortunately, they are also stories from the present. In less time than it will take you to read just one chapter of this book, five Christians will be martyred for their faith. That is a true and yet sobering statistic, and one that for most of us, we rarely have to acknowledge. We can worship freely and have access to God's Word in any form we choose. It's easy to forget our brothers and sisters around the world and what they endure each and every day.

The following pages will take you on a journey to the frontlines of the persecuted church. Your eyes will be opened, your sense of justice attacked, and your heart stretched. But my hope is that when you put this book down, your journey will not stop. Because in the words of the famous abolitionist William Wilberforce, "You can choose to look the other way, but you can never say again that you did not know."

I believe the question you will be left with is simple: What will you choose to do?

The world has changed so much since World Help started 30 years ago, but our mission has not. And as long as there are people persecuted for their faith and spiritually starved, without access to God's Word, we will continue our fight. I invite you to join us.

Noel Brewer Yeatts
President, World Help

PROLOGUE

I met Ping several years ago on a trip to Vietnam. Her story of persecution is the kind that haunts you for days and weeks later. In some respects, it still haunts me today.

I'll never forget the look on her face as she recounted the abuse and torture she had endured for being a faithful follower of Jesus Christ.

This 34-year-old woman had once been a Buddhist and lived in a monastery. She had been sick for many years. When Ping accepted Christ, she was immediately healed from her disease.

She is now an evangelist and church planter. When I met her, she had started six churches and had 47 more new churches developing.

One day, Ping's husband was asked by a new convert to help him destroy his family's ancestral altar. An informant turned them in, and the police videotaped them. The two men were arrested, and Ping's husband was sent to prison for months. She was left alone with her young children.

This young woman had been arrested six times by the secret police. She suffered continuous persecution. She was beaten numerous times, detained for weeks at a time, and fined the equivalent of $250, which is six months' salary. The police beat her on the head every day for two weeks ... she almost died.

When she survived, they decided to tie her hands

together and throw her overboard from a boat in the river. Once again, she miraculously survived. The police then forced her to march up and down a mountain for days.

She said when she could no longer stand the beatings, she would pray and ask God for strength.

One day the police publicly humiliated her by tearing off her shirt and parading her through the streets. She stood in that public gathering, half naked, with her hands tied behind her back, and said:

"I live for Jesus Christ.
If I die … I die for Jesus Christ!"

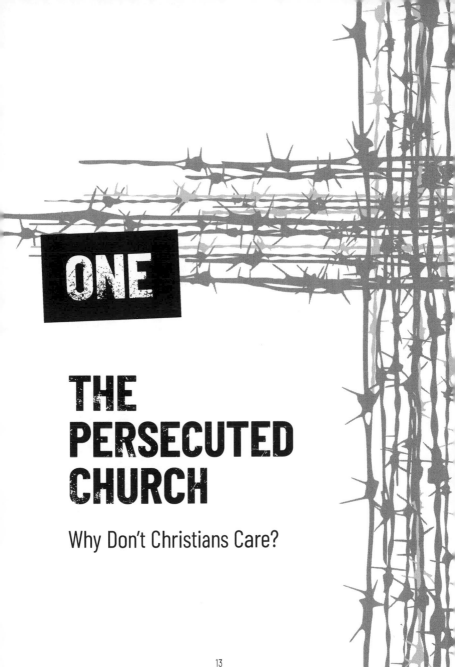

ONE

THE
PERSECUTED
CHURCH

Why Don't Christians Care?

Dear brothers and sisters, when troubles of any kind come your way, consider it an opportunity for great joy. For you know that when your faith is tested, your endurance has a chance to grow.   — JAMES 1:2-3

D ietrick Bonhoeffer, a German Lutheran pastor wrote these words in 1937: *"When Christ calls a man, He bids him come and die."* How could he have known that he himself would be hanged in a Nazi concentration camp ... his only crime ... he was a Christian.

The persecution of Christians around the world is more severe than ever. Because of communism, the 20th century saw more martyrs than in the previous 19 centuries combined.

- In Sudan, Christians are enslaved. In Iran, they are assassinated. ln Cuba, they are imprisoned. In China, they are beaten to death.
- In more than 60 countries worldwide, Christians are harassed, abused, arrested, tortured, or executed specifically for following Jesus Christ.
- It is estimated that every 5 minutes a Christian is killed for their faith.[1]
- An average of 105,000 believers are killed each year

for simply being a Christian.[2]
- That means in the past ten years we've seen more than 1 million martyrs.

These are not wild rumors. Nor are these simply Christians who suffer from war or tyranny. Hundreds of millions of Christians are suffering simply because of what they believe.[3]

In many ways Jesus himself was the first martyr and most of His disciples and followers suffered cruel and agonizing deaths.

- Stephen was stoned to death.
- James, son of Zebedee, was beheaded.
- Philip was scourged, thrown into prison, and then crucified.
- Matthew was slain with an ax.
- James the Less was beaten, stoned, and finally had his brains dashed out.
- Matthias was stoned and beheaded.
- Andrew was crucified on an X-shaped cross.
- Mark was dragged to pieces.
- Peter was crucified upside down.
- Paul gave his neck to the sword.
- Jude was crucified.
- Bartholomew was cruelly beaten and crucified.
- Thomas was thrust through with a spear.
- Luke was hanged on an olive tree.
- Simon was crucified.

- John, the "beloved disciple," was the only apostle who escaped a violent death.[4]

THE MARTYRDOM OF STEPHEN

Acts 6:8-15

[8]Stephen, a man full of God's grace and power, performed amazing miracles and signs among the people. [9]But one day some men from the Synagogue started to debate with him. [10]None of them could stand against the wisdom and the Spirit with which Stephen spoke.

[11]So they persuaded some men to lie about Stephen, saying, "We heard him blaspheme Moses, and even God." [12]This roused the people, the elders, and the teachers of religious law. So they arrested Stephen and brough him before the high council.

[13]The lying witnesses said, "This man is always speaking against the holy Temple and against the law of Moses. [14]We have heard him say that this Jesus of Nazareth will destroy the Temple and change the customs Moses handed down to us."

[15]At this point everyone in the high council stared at Stephen, because his face became as bright as an angel's.

Acts 7:51-59

[51]"You stubborn people! You are heathen at heart and deaf to the truth. Must you forever resist the Holy Spirit? That's what your ancestors did, and so do you! [52]Name one prophet your ancestors didn't persecute! They even killed the ones who predicted the coming of the Righteous One – the Messiah whom you betrayed and murdered. [53]You deliberately disobeyed God's law, even though you received it from the hands of angels."

[54]The Jewish leaders were infuriated by Stephen's accusation, and they shook their fists at him in rage. [55]But Stephen, full of the Holy Spirit, gazed steadily into heaven and saw the glory of God, and he saw Jesus standing in the place of honor at God's right hand. [56]And he told them, "Look, I see the heavens opened and the Son of Man standing in the place of honor at God's right hand!"

[57]Then they put their hands over their ears and began shouting. They rushed at him [58]and dragged him out of the city and began to stone him. His accusers took off their coats and laid them at the feet of a young man named Saul.

[59]As they stoned him, Stephen prayed, "Lord Jesus, receive my spirit."

Acts 8:1-3
Saul was one of the witnesses, and he agreed completely with the killing of Stephen. A great wave of persecution began that day, sweeping over the church in Jerusalem; and all the believers except the apostles were scattered through the regions of Judea and Samaria. 2 (Some devout men came and buried Stephen with great mourning.) 3 But Saul was going everywhere to destroy the church. He went from house to house, dragging out both men and women to throw them into prison.

"*Christian persecution did not stop with the deaths of the apostles. It has continued throughout the centuries and grown dramatically in the past few decades. From a spiritual viewpoint, we shouldn't be surprised. The devil still 'prowls around like a roaring lion, looking for someone to devour.' He still seeks to snuff out the life of Jesus in all who call upon His name. Yet persecution's visible causes are varied. The attacks can be indirect and subtle, or violent and deadly. But make no mistake: Christian persecution is increasing and one way or another it affects us all.*"[5]

Mark Batterson in the introduction of his book, *Play the Man*, tells the gripping story of the martyrdom of Polycarp, one of the early church fathers.

THE MARTYRDOM OF POLYCARP

Let us play the men for our people.
—2 Samuel 10:12 KJV

February 23, AD 155
Smyrna, Greece

"Like a scene straight out of *Gladiator*, Polycarp was dragged into the Roman Colosseum. Discipled by the Apostle John himself, the aged bishop faithfully and selflessly led the church at Smyrna through the persecution prophesied by his spiritual father. 'Do not be afraid of what you are about to suffer,' writes John in Revelation 2:10. 'Be faithful, even to the point of death.'

John had died a half century before, but his voice still echoed in Polycarp's ears as the Colosseum crowd chanted, 'Let loose the lion!' That's when Polycarp heard a voice from heaven that was audible above the crowd.

'Be strong, Polycarp. Play the man.'

Days before, Roman bounty hunters had tracked him down. Instead of fleeing, Polycarp fed them a meal. Perhaps that's why they granted his last request – an hour of prayer. Two hours later, many of those who heard the way Polycarp prayed actually repented of their sin on the spot. They did not, however, relent of their mission.

Like Jesus entering Jerusalem, Polycarp was led into the city of Smyrna on a donkey. The Roman proconsul implored Polycarp to recant. 'Swear by the genius of Caesar!'

Polycarp held his tongue, held his ground. The proconsul prodded, 'Swear, and I will release thee; revile the Christ!'

'Eighty and six years have I served Him,' said Polycarp. 'And He has done me no wrong! How then can I blaspheme my King who saved me?'

The die was cast.

Polycarp was led to the center of the Colosseum where three times the proconsul announced, 'Polycarp has confessed himself to be a Christian.' The bloodthirsty crowd chanted for death by beast, but the proconsul opted for fire.

As his executioners seized his wrists to nail him to the stake, Polycarp stopped them. 'He who gives me strength to endure the fire will enable me to do so without the help of your nails.'

As the pyre was lit on fire, Polycarp prayed one last prayer. 'I bless you because you have thought me worthy of this day and this hour to be numbered among your martyrs in the cup of your Christ.' Soon the flames engulfed him, but strangely they did not consume him. Like Shadrach, Meshach, and Abednego before him, Polycarp was fireproof. Instead of the stench of burning flesh, the scent of frankincense wafted through the Colosseum.

Using a spear, the executioner stabbed Polycarp through the flames. Polycarp bled out, but not before the twelfth martyr of Smyrna had lived out John's exhortation: be faithful even to the point of death. Polycarp died fearlessly and faithfully. And the way he died forever changed the way those eyewitnesses lived. He did what the voice from heaven had commanded. Polycarp played the man."[6]

It seems that every day we hear another news story of a church that is attacked, a missionary who is held hostage, or a Christian who has been murdered for their faith.

And with today's technology, persecution has now gone digital. Governments are increasingly using surveillance to target Christians, particularly in China and India. By using facial-recognition technology and artificial intelligence, leaders can identify and discriminate against believers.[7]

BUT WHY IS IT THAT SO MANY CHRISTIANS JUST DON'T CARE?

One leader working with the persecuted church gives two reasons for Christians' relative lack of interest in the plight of suffering sisters and brothers worldwide:

- "American Christians, for the most part, are not interested in anything that happens outside the boundaries of the United States, and in many cases outside the boundaries of their own community ..."[8]
- "American Christians have no experience of persecution or suffering for their faith that remotely resembles the experiences of many of our overseas brothers and sisters. It is difficult to empathize ... many, many, many American Christians refuse to believe what is reported because it is so far outside their experience."[9]

I admit, at first, I had a hard time believing some of the stories of persecution that I heard and read about. Things like that just don't happen ... too horrible to comprehend.

But I have seen the actual scars. I have heard the heartache and sorrow in their voices. I have seen the suffering in their eyes. It's an unforgettable picture that is etched in my heart and in my mind forever. And I hope that God never allows me to forget!

Although we live in a world of disbelief and mistrust, we as Christians cannot afford to be skeptics about persecution. Persecution is real and it is happening all around us.

PERSECUTION STATISTICS

In 2020, **4,488** churches or Christian buildings were attacked; **4,277** Christians were detained without trial, arrested, sentenced, or imprisoned.

Around the world, more than **340 MILLION** Christians live in places where they experience high levels of persecution, just for following Jesus. That's 1 in 8 believers worldwide.

An average of **13** Christians is killed each day because of their faith.

This number is likely much lower than the actual reality because in closed countries like North Korea and Afghanistan, or conflict-ridden places like Nigeria and Libya, killings are often done in secrecy and go unreported.

Source: Open Doors

In the year 67 AD, Christians living under Nero's rule, the sixth emperor of Rome, suffered some of the worst forms of persecution. They were sewn into the skin of wild animals and fed to wild dogs. Some were even covered with wax and made into human candles that were used to light Nero's garden.[10]

The history of the church is full of courageous and bold witnesses who have glorified Christ in their death for Him — John Huss, Thomas Cranmer, Hugh Latimer, William Tyndale — burned at the stake for the sake of the Gospel.

At the height of communism, it is estimated that nearly a half million Christians were killed every year. Many Christians in China today still suffer under the hand of communism and risk their lives simply to own a Bible.[11]

"Evidence shows not only the geographic spread of anti-Christian persecution, but also its increasing severity. In some regions, the level and nature of persecution is arguably coming close to meeting the international definition of genocide ..."[12]

These stories of horrendous persecution and suffering should shake us to our very being. This is not make-believe. This is not a book of fiction. This is not sensationalism created for an upcoming movie! These are actual, very graphic, and unbelievable accounts of persecution. This is reality!

We should be on our knees every day thanking God that this is not what we must endure daily. We should thank God that we don't have to watch our wives, husbands, sons, and daughters suffer immense pain and anguish, and possibly even death, just for their faith.

But how are we as Christians to respond to a persecuted church? Does persecution really affect us? What is our responsibility and what can we learn from it? How can we embrace a suffering church?

Someone suggested that when trying to make sense of persecution and martyrdom, four key reasons are usually given:

Persecution purifies the church. There are no nominal believers in the persecuted church. There are no Sunday morning Christians in the persecuted church. There are no casual Christians in the persecuted church.

Persecution unifies the church. There are no disputes over minor doctrinal issues in the persecuted church. There are no struggles for power in the persecuted church.

Persecution strengthens the church. Believers in the persecuted church are courageous and bold because every day they are compelled to take a stand for Jesus Christ.

Persecution grows the church. In 1950, when communism took over in China and missionaries were expelled, there were only 1 million Christians in the entire country. Today, even the government recognizes that there are at least 44 million Christians in China; some estimate that it could be as high as 130 million. The reason we do not know for sure is that many of them are meeting secretly in house churches.

It was even suggested that the best thing that could happen to the church in America would be for you and me to experience real persecution.[13]

One of the most famous martyrs of our time was Jim Elliot. I was 10 years old when I realized what a martyr was. I saw the bodies of five slain missionaries on the cover of *LIFE* magazine.

Before being murdered by a remote tribe of Indians in South America that he was trying to reach with the Gospel,

But I have seen the actual scars. I have heard the heartache and sorrow in their voices. I have seen the suffering in their eyes. It's an unforgettable picture that is etched in my heart and in my mind forever. And I hope that God never allows me to forget!

Jim Elliot wrote in his journal, "I seek not a long life, but a full one, like you, Lord Jesus ... I must not think it strange if God takes in youth those whom I would have kept on earth till they were older. God is peopling Eternity, and I must not restrict Him to old men and women."

He also wrote these words that are now famous, "He is no fool, who gives what he cannot keep to gain what he cannot lose."

God will not call most of us to be martyrs or to face severe persecution. But God does call each one of us to be "living sacrifices."

"In some respects, it may be harder to live for Christ than to die for Him; but if we are living for Him, we will be prepared to die for Him if that is what God calls us to do."[14]

If believers in India, China, Vietnam, and all around the world are willing to die for Jesus Christ, surely, we should be willing to live for Jesus Christ!

"How many more Christians will have to suffer and die before we realize that it is our job to try to stop these atrocities? We are often so caught up with our own petty problems that we don't make time to think about the Christians who are bleeding and dying across the world."

— Luis Palau

Christians in the West have come a long way in believing that persecution truly exists — that people are actually dying just for believing in Jesus Christ. We are educating ourselves and seeking ways to help the persecuted church.

But there is so much more to be done. So many needs ...

- They need to have training to plant churches. In India alone, there are over 500,000 villages and cities without a church of any kind. We must train leaders and church planters.
- They need to have buildings in which to meet. The Hindus say to Christians in Asia, "If your God is so great, why don't you have a place to worship Him?"
- They need Bibles. In China, there are still millions of Christians who have never held a Bible, let alone owned one. And we can do something about that!

- They need prayer. Nothing of eternal significance is ever accomplished apart from prayer. We must be mobilized to pray for the persecuted church.
- They need us to follow their example.

"God uses the suffering of His missionaries to awaken others out of their slumbers of indifference and make them bold ... If He must, God will use the suffering of His devoted emissaries to make a sleeping church wake up and take risks for God."[15]

The persecuted church does not understand our lifestyle. The persecuted church does not understand our materialism, selfishness, and prayerlessness.

It's a mystery to them how they can have so very little, and love God so very much ... and we have so very much and appear to love God so very little.

Johnnie Moore, my good friend, and World Help board member, in a recent article for CBN News, underscores

"First-century persecution in the 21st-century — while horrific and evil — is also producing a first-century harvest of millions coming to follow Jesus in the most miraculous ways and from the most unlikely places."

— Johnnie Moore

why every believer should be concerned about the global persecution of Christians today. He states: "Christians are being persecuted around the world at a pace not seen since the first century."

Johnnie also serves as one of nine commissioners appointed to the U.S. Commission on International Religious Freedom (USCIRF).

The 2021 USCIRF reports that:

- **50,000 Christians** are being held in North Korean prison camps
- Some **3,000 Yazidi girls and women** are missing in Iraq
- **130,000 Muslims** are confined in internment camps in Myanmar (Burma)
- As many as **3 million Uighur Muslims** are being held in Chinese concentration camps

The report also identifies countries of particular concern, which are the worst offenders.

Ten of those are already designated as such by the State Department: Myanmar (Burma), China, Eritrea, Iran, Nigeria, North Korea, Pakistan, Saudi Arabia, Tajikistan, and Turkmenistan.

The USCIRF recommends adding India, Russia, Syria, and Vietnam to the list.

"It's time for Christians to do what the Apostle Paul called them to do," Johnnie continued, "which is to pray for those who are in prison as if they were there with them."

In his book, *"The Martyr's Oath – Living for the Jesus They're Willing to Die For,"* Johnnie stated, "if you follow Jesus, there's a part of your family you need to know: those who are suffering and those who will die for Jesus.

I wonder how many of us in the United States have counted the cost of following Jesus – I mean *really* counted the cost. For some, we may think we have. We just don't think we need Jesus very much.

Jesus is the ultimate 'value add' to whatever version of the good life we fashioned, the capstone to a life well lived. He gives unilateral approval to our decisions and may get us out of a jam now and then, but He doesn't require much from us. We don't demand much of him, so he can't demand much of us.

"But we also need their help. For all that we may be doing to help them, they also help us. They inspire us to a deeper place in our commitment to Jesus. They inspire us to *live* for the Jesus they are willing to die for. Their testimonies call us to take our own faith more seriously, and they lead us to discover the true power of Jesus."[16]

The stories you read in this book are compelling. They are true. And persecuted Christians need our help.

FROM MY PRAYER JOURNAL

God, you have my attention. Help me to see and feel their suffering so very real in my own life that I cannot forget what I have seen and felt. I can't even begin to imagine what these dear Christians suffer daily; they are sacrificing so much for you. My faith and commitment pales by comparison. Never let me become complacent and comfortable again. Thank you for refocusing my attention on what is really important in this life and what really matters.

Amen

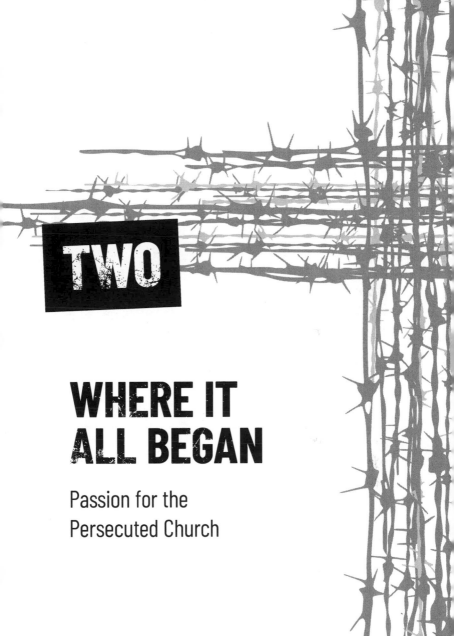

TWO

WHERE IT ALL BEGAN

Passion for the
Persecuted Church

Yes, everything else is worthless when compared with the infinite value of knowing Christ Jesus my Lord. For his sake I have discarded everything else, counting it all as garbage, so that I could gain Christ.   — PHILIPPIANS 3:8

My journey with the persecuted church began in the early 1980s on my first visit to Romania. At the time, that country was experiencing the tyranny of a communist dictatorship. I was struck by the believers I met who, despite living under harsh conditions and being almost destitute, remained steadfast in their faith and love for God.

I was detained at the border and my camera, Bible, and sermon notes were confiscated. I never got them back. We were followed by the secret police everywhere we went, and after we left, the Romanian pastors we visited were arrested and interrogated — only because we had been there.

Despite great persecution, we found Christ-followers who were totally committed to Jesus Christ. They attended early morning prayer meetings and packed into the outdated church buildings five times a week. Hundreds stood in the aisles. They had so little, but they loved God so much.

One church I visited was scheduled for bulldozing by the government supposedly to make room for a high-rise apartment building, but really as harassment and persecution. Soldiers were sent to make sure the building was demolished. The night before it was scheduled for demolition, the congregation locked themselves in the church building and prayed all night. Amazingly, the next day the soldiers left, and the building was saved.

A few months later, Billy Graham spoke at that same church. There were more than 35,000 people inside the building and overflowing into the streets just to hear him preach.

"I WILL NOT DO WHAT YOU ASK"

On June 12, 1987, President Ronald Reagan stood at the Berlin Wall, the defining symbol of the Cold War, and spoke these words, which are now famous: "Mr. Gorbachev, tear down this wall."

Only two years later, the once unthinkable happened. The wall came down.

I was in Budapest, Hungary, with a group of 57 Liberty University students as it was happening. We boarded the train to Oradea, Romania, a five-hour ride. For most of the students, it would be their first visit to a communist country.

When we arrived at the Romanian border, we were detained. Our car was detached from the train and placed on a different track. We sat there for more than 14 hours without food, water, or heat. Many of the students were frightened, to say the least.

The former Soviet Union was unraveling, and Romanian dictator Nicolae Ceausescu didn't want what was happening in Moscow and Berlin to happen in Romania. He ordered Romania's borders closed to all foreigners. We were stuck.

After a cold night, workers reattached our train car to an outbound train, and we were on our way back to Budapest. As we pulled out of the station, one of the girls was crying. I asked her if she was sad because she could not visit Romania. "No," she said, 'I'm sad because I now see the persecution that the Romanian people live with every day."

On my next visit early one Sunday morning, my friend Pastor Cornel Iova picked me up in his car. We were going to visit a village church several hours away in the mountains.

As I sat in the back seat, Cornel said, "Today is a very special day for me." When I asked why, he replied, "Today is the first anniversary of the death of my wife." Sympathetically, I asked how she died.

"Cancer," he said. He knew I was a cancer survivor.

He told me his wife was diagnosed by a group of doctors who had visited Romania from the United Kingdom. They offered to bring her to London to perform the delicate bone marrow transplant surgery that could not be done in Romania at the time. They would pay for all the expenses. All she needed was a visa to leave the country.

When she went to the government office to apply for the visa, they already knew she was a pastor's wife. The communist authorities told her they would give her a visa only if she renounced her faith in Jesus Christ. I was shocked.

"What did she say?" I asked.

"She didn't hesitate for one instant. She responded, 'I cannot, and I will not do what you ask me to do,'" Cornel said. "With her head held high, she walked out of that office."

A few minutes later, he added, "Within two months she was gone."

"I'm sad because I now see the persecution that the Romanian people live with every day."

I could not comprehend that level of commitment. I had no idea what to say. I simply told him how sorry I was.

After several moments of silence, he added, "Today is a special day for another reason." He explained that the village we were visiting was conducting their first baptismal service in more than 50 years.

In fact, the government had sent soldiers to demolish the church three times, and all three times the church members rebuilt the building. Cornel told me there would be 21 candidates for baptism, and that I would share the Gospel with the entire village.

When we arrived, I found the church packed to capacity. All the family members of the baptismal candidates were there and almost everyone in the village was present. Some of the youth wired the houses of villagers with closed circuit TV so those who were unable to attend could view the service.

Cornel was right. I preached the Gospel to the entire village. That day we saw more than 62 new Christ-followers, and that remote Romanian village was changed forever.

A few months later, I was back in Romania. I was invited to speak at the Communist Congress Palace in Bucharest where dictators ruled with an iron fist. The place was packed that night with more than 4,000 people and most of them had never heard the Gospel. Before the night was over, 300 became Christ-followers.

Since my first trip to Romania, I have visited at least 38 times. I never realized then what I know full well now. This country was on the brink of revolution and unprecedented religious freedom. The walls were torn down. The world would never be the same.

FROM MY PRAYER JOURNAL

Oh, God ... You have touched my
heart as only You can do.
Thank you!

Thank you for introducing me
to dedicated pastors, church
planters, and evangelists that are
doing an incredible work for You.
Bless them I pray.

Thank you for allowing me the
incredible opportunity to be in the
presence of your humble servants
who have been beaten, tortured,
arrested, and imprisoned.

Don't let me avoid persecution.
Change the way I live, the way I
view life, the way I spend money.
Let me live more with You in
focus.

Thank you for showing me how we can help them. Please don't let me close my eyes to this great opportunity but open my heart to what You want me to do.

Thank you for prolonging my life ... for healing me of cancer ... for allowing me to serve You.

Lord, never again let me feel sorry for myself because of some minor trial or inconvenience.

Thank you for breaking my heart with the things that break Your heart! Please don't ever let me be the same again!

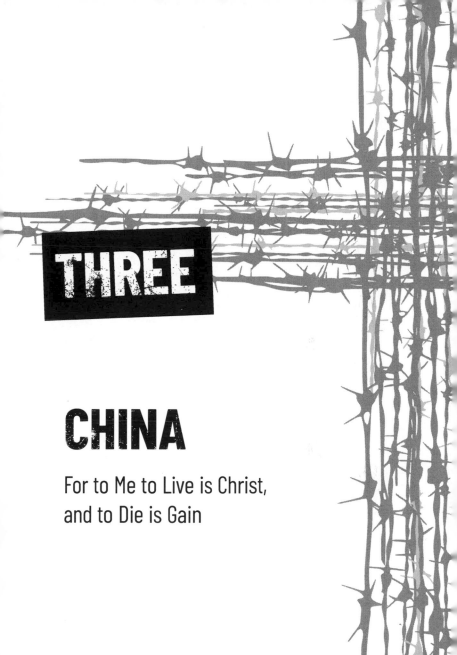

THREE

CHINA

For to Me to Live is Christ,
and to Die is Gain

2021 WORLD WATCH LIST

Rank: #17
Persecution type: Communist and post-communist oppression
Religion: Agnosticism
Persecution level: High
Population: 1,424,548,000
Christian: 97,200,000
Government: Communist state

Source: Open Doors

CHINA

God blesses those who are persecuted for doing right, for the Kingdom of Heaven is theirs. God blesses you when people mock you and persecute you and lie about you and say all sorts of evil things against you because you are my followers. Be happy about it! Be very glad! For a great reward awaits you in heaven. And remember, the ancient prophets were persecuted in the same way.   — MATTHEW 5:10-12

A s I stepped into the taxi, I pulled a crumpled sheet of paper out of my pocket. On it was written an address in both English and Cantonese: 35 Da Ma Zhan.

In Guangzhou, a city of over 3 million people, I was alone and had no idea where I was going. My goal was to meet one of China's most well-known house church leaders, Lin Xiangao, who also used the Western name, Samuel Lamb. He pastored Da Ma Zhan Church, one of the largest house churches in China.

When the Chinese taxi driver stopped in the middle of the street, I said, "No, no," and once again pointed to the small sheet of paper. He nodded yes and pointed me in the direction of a small alley, barely 20 feet wide. "Da Ma Zhan," he said.

It was nearly dark, and the alley was packed with people. Families sat outside their doorways, mothers cooked rice, and older men — wearing their blue Mao jackets — played Mah-Jongg, a Chinese game that looked a lot like Dominos to me. The smells of fish, steamed rice, and vegetables filled the air. I felt I had stepped back in time.

Walking down the alley, I felt a little intimidated, but I had come too far to let fear stop me. I arrived at number 35 — a small, three-story apartment building — and as I expected, uniformed armed guards met me. They occupied the first floor, guarding Pastor Lamb who was under house arrest.

He had endured more than 21 years in prison for his faith because he would not register his church with the Chinese government. Fifteen of those years, he had done hard physical labor in a coal mine after he tried to make a handwritten copy of the New Testament.

While Pastor Lamb was in prison, his wife died, but the authorities never bothered to give him the news. Eleven months later, his mother — who also was living in their home — passed away.

After his eventual release, he returned to his apartment and learned of their deaths. He was placed under house arrest and was not allowed to leave his apartment building without permission from the police.

I was eager to meet Pastor Lamb. His house church meeting had just dismissed, so I had to wait outside while hundreds of Chinese believers made their way down the narrow staircase and filed past me into the night. I had to push past the guards to make my way up the stairs. When I reached the third floor, I met my hero for the first time.

Pastor Lamb was short — I towered over him. With a contagious smile, he invited me to come in. The first thing I remember seeing was a long table with about 20 Chinese young people writing feverishly. Nearly 80 percent of the pastor's congregation is young people hungry for the Word of God and eager to share it with their friends.

I asked Pastor Lamb what they were doing. He matter-of-factly explained, "They are making handwritten copies of the Gospel of John to give to their friends at school tomorrow. We only have one Bible at this time, so we must make copies."

I thought to myself, "This would never happen in my country. Most Christian young people in America would never think of giving a Gospel of John to their friends in school, let alone make a handwritten copy."

As I sat there with this leader of the house church movement, he told me his stories and showed me his photos and an official Oval Office pen from Ronald Reagan. It was a gift from a White House staff member who told him, "President Reagan told me to ask you to pray for him whenever you use this pen."

He showed me a photo of Billy Graham standing behind the makeshift pulpit in that Da Ma Zhan apartment. As I looked around, I noticed the walls had been knocked out and replaced with wooden benches. In the far corner was a single bed, a small refrigerator, and a hot plate — Pastor Lamb's living space. Every single inch of the rest of the apartment was converted to a meeting room for the Da Ma Zhan Church.

Pastor Lamb said he started preaching again when he was released from prison, and his house church started growing. One day, concerned authorities stormed into the meeting and arrested Pastor Lamb again. They confiscated all the Bibles and hymnals. For three days, he was interrogated, beaten, and tortured. He was told to go back and close the Da Ma Zhan house church.

"What did you do?" I asked.

China is home to one of the largest populations of religious prisoners, likely numbering in the tens of thousands; while in custody, some are tortured or killed, rights groups say. Instances of arbitrary detentions and violence carried out with impunity have led the U.S. State Department to designate China as a country of particular concern over religious freedom annually since 1999.[17]

"I stood in the church the next week," he said, "and told the congregation that the police said not to come back."

"What happened?"

"The next Sunday," he said, "our church attendance doubled. Jesus said, 'Upon this rock I will build my church; and the gates of hell shall not prevail against it.'"[18]

At the time, Da Ma Zhan Church was one of the largest

house churches in China. Every week, more than 1,500 believers packed into five services.

"How did you survive all those years in prison?" I asked.

"I quoted Scripture I had committed to memory and composed hymns to worship God," he said. His two favorite biblical passages were written from prison to the Christians at Philippi and to young Timothy:

> *Don't worry about anything; instead, pray about everything. Tell God what you need, and thank him for all he has done. Then you will experience God's peace, which exceeds anything we can understand. His peace will guard your hearts and minds as you live in Christ Jesus. (Philippians 4:6-7)*

> *I have fought the good fight, I have finished the race, and I have remained faithful. And now the prize awaits me — the crown of righteousness, which the Lord, the righteous Judge, will give me on the day of his return. And the prize is not just for me but for all who eagerly look forward to his appearing.*
> *(2 Timothy 4:7-8)*

"Pray for us dearly, because we don't know about tomorrow," Pastor Lamb said. "We don't know when tribulation will come. Pray that our people might have strength to face persecution. They are threatened by the government with no salary or job if they attend the meetings, yet they still come. **But please do not pray for the**

persecution to stop."

His last statement took me by surprise, but then I realized he saw persecution as a blessing. Every time they arrested him and sent him to prison, the church grew.

I asked Pastor Lamb how I could help him. He asked me to bring them more Bibles.

Over the years, I visited him many times, each time bringing him a load of Bibles — sometimes sending them ahead in vans, and sometimes not even telling him their source.

But still, every time I visited that special house church, I looked around and saw only a few Bibles — the need was so great. People crowded around and peered over the shoulders of those who held the Bibles, just to follow along as the Word of God was read aloud.

On many occasions, I saw people holding torn pieces of paper. I soon realized these were pages from a Bible and shared in the group. This was not done out of disrespect for God's Word, but for the unquenchable desire to have a small portion of their very own.

On one of my visits, Pastor Lamb said the Public Security Bureau — the secret police — questioned him about my visit. They asked, "Why are you meeting with foreigners?"

"I am not," he said. "He is my brother."

One of the highlights of my life was one Sunday when Pastor Lamb invited me to speak to the Da Ma Zhan house church. He was my interpreter.

I was blessed to call Pastor Lamb my friend. He endured

more persecution than anyone I know. He was beaten and tortured for his faith — and yet he never wavered. Every time I was with him, he had a smile on his face and a song in his heart. He was God's gift to the underground church in China.

Samuel Lamb may have been small in stature, but he was a giant of the faith to me.[19]

GUILTY OF BELIEVING IN GOD

I remember the day I read this letter from a Christian woman who is in prison in China. Her story and passion moved me deeply.

My name is Guizhen Zhang. I am a 43-year-old woman. One night my family was sleeping, and I was awakened by a loud noise in the yard. I turned on the light, and a group of people suddenly broke in and started ransacking the house. One of them yelled at me, "Get up now, and come with us." I asked him, "What crime did I commit?" "You'll know when the time comes." Then they pushed and pulled my husband (Yuejin Li) and me by force into their police car and took us to the police station.

The next day I was taken to the detention house to be interrogated by four people. "Do you know why you were arrested?" "No, I don't," I replied. One of them yelled back fiercely, "It is because of you believing in God. (He cursed at me.) You're so stubborn, you deserve a good beating."

With this, he slapped me hard several times. I was so dizzy that I was seeing stars, and my ears were ringing. He shouted at me while he was slapping me, "Kneel down!" He kicked me and knocked me down to the floor. "Are you going to tell us why you believe in God? Shameless woman, you're worthless running around here to there."

They forced me to raise my cuffed hands up for more than an hour. Whenever I couldn't hold up my arms any longer and they fell, the police would kick at my waist, hit my head hard, twist my ears, and pull my hair. My hair was pulled out and my ears hurt so bad as if they were cut by a knife. I began to scream. However, they didn't stop their interrogation.

Four of them kept cursing and beating me for more than three hours till I was lying on the floor motionless like dead, black and blue all over. Even so, they still didn't stop torturing me.

The torture lasted till it was getting dark when they let me go back to the cell. My cell is closed all day with a disgusting smell because the inmates were not allowed to leave and use the toilet. It is not a place for human beings. In the morning and evening, we are only given a bowl of watery noodle soup and a half-steamed bread. At noon we get cabbage boiled in water: I am starved every day.

Three days later, I was sentenced to two years, and I am currently serving out my term. I was accused of "Believing in God." I remain guilty.

Guizhen Zhang[20]

I was so stunned after reading this letter I quietly prayed, Dear God, may I always remain guilty of believing in you!

TORTURED, BURIED ALIVE

Christians are tortured regularly in China simply for believing in Jesus Christ. One Chinese Christian wrote:

"One of my mother's coworkers, a pastor, was caught by the communist officials. They tortured and beat him, trying to make him renounce his faith. He would not do it. At last, they became so angry with him that they brought a coffin and made him lie in it. They told him 'All right, now we want you to make a final decision; either deny Christ, or we will bury you.' His only reply was, 'I will never deny my Lord.' They nailed the coffin shut and left it sitting for a time, listening for a voice from the inside. There was none. They screamed and shouted at him and pounded on the casket. Still, only the sound of quiet,

contented breathing could be heard. **They buried him alive."**

Other reported methods of torture in China include hanging men and women upside down, squeezing them under chairs, exposing them to extreme weather conditions for extended periods, and burning their tongues with electric probes to prevent them from invoking aloud God's help.

A group of underground Christians, caught with Bibles, suffered crippling beatings by the police ... they can no longer walk without assistance. Others were tortured by having their heels stomped on while they were kneeling.

When a pastor refused to cooperate with the Chinese secret police by giving names of other Christian leaders, they used a pair of pliers to squeeze the ends of his fingers until they broke, and he passed out.

Two young women were hung from the rafters by their thumbs and stripped naked by the guards. They were beaten with rods until they fell unconscious. They then served three years in a labor camp.

After their release, the women courageously returned to preaching the Gospel, moving from one town to the next, spending only one week in each locality to not attract attention from the police. When asked what they would do if they were discovered again, they replied, "We would welcome it as another opportunity to share with them the love of Jesus."

"PERSECUTION IS NORMAL FOR US"

I received this letter written by a Chinese Christian:

We have heard a rumor that overseas people are saying that there is no longer any persecution in China. We find this hard to believe. There are more than 100 pastors in prison here, and many young Christians under 18 are under strong pressure from the police. Some were thrown in manure pits, others were beaten with electric stun batons, some were beaten so they could not stand.

Persecution is normal for us.

Overseas, Christians say that the Gospel is flourishing in China because people have lost faith in Marxism and because of material poverty. These are certainly reasons. But I believe deeply that we have paid a great price for the Gospel — much blood and sweat and many tears.

The Word of God is held in great esteem and highly cherished among house church Christians. Bibles are still very scarce in some areas and there is a great hunger among the people of God for the Scriptures.

It is not merely for the pleasure of being able to read the Bible that we long to own a copy. We are desperate to understand God's heart on many issues.

We want to be doers of the Word, not merely hearers.

Bibles are like gold dust, virtually unobtainable for many Christians. That is why portions of the Scripture are still copied out by hand, many times over, and distributed to as many people as possible. These portions will sometimes be memorized thoroughly. You discover just how much has been remembered when we pray — for the Word of God is liberally mixed into our prayers.

Chinese Christians love God's Word. We will travel hundreds of miles to obtain a copy of the Bible.

We will go for long distances by foot or bicycle just to hear an itinerant evangelist preach. Once we are in a meeting, we drink in the Word of God. We are more than happy to sit and listen for hour upon hour. Often, we will not let preachers stop, but encourage them to give all that they have, until the preachers are exhausted.

One pastor recounts a visit he made to the city to meet a relatively new convert who had begged him to let her do something for God in a way of distributing Bibles and tapes. He was due to meet her at 9 p.m., but she did not arrive until 1 a.m. She was delayed because she had been delivering some Bibles in a village not far from their meeting place.

The local authorities had discovered what she was doing and had beat her up, robbed her, and left her on a deserted road. Still, she kept her appointment with the pastor.

Apart from the beating, she did not look at all well. When the pastor asked what was wrong with her, she showed him her legs that were covered with stings and mosquito bites. This was part of her price for traveling in remote parts of the countryside delivering God's Word.

She had to sleep in huts or open fields, attacked by many insects. He urged her to go to the doctor with him, but she refused. She explained that she had to leave the next morning for Inner Mongolia with the Bibles that he had brought her.

Not long after that she disappeared, and nothing was heard from her for some time. Later, the pastor received a small piece of paper smuggled through by some friends of hers. On it was written the news that she had been arrested and charged with "distributing superstitious materials."

A few weeks later, news filtered through that this 24-year-old young woman, who had given all her energy to delivering the Word of God so desperately needed by Christians, had been executed. She had been able to answer the question in the affirmative: The Word of God was worth dying for.[21]

"SNOWMAN" SURVIVES FRIGID PERSECUTION

My lifelong friend, Tom Thompson, shared with me a moving story of a pastor he met in China.

"I'll never forget the day I met Pastor Enoch. However, he is called, 'Snowman.' Allow me to explain why.

Born in 1969, Enoch came to Christ some time in 1984. During those early days in his new faith, he did not understand all that he embraced because there was no Bible available for him to read.

At the age of 15, he felt a call of God to ministry. Though not educated or having Bible training, he wasn't afraid of anything. Even as a young man, God used him to influence not only his hometown, but also the surrounding provinces in spreading the Gospel. It was all by the grace and power of Christ.

As a result of this early work, he is one of the founders of the early house church movements in China. But Enoch faced constant and severe persecution.

The result – sometimes for several years at a time.

In 1985, he obtained his first copy of a Bible. I'm told by our Chinese partner that, 'During those days there weren't many copies of the Bible, and so he got his co-workers and congregation members together and they would read the Bible aloud together and go through the entire Bible in six to seven days, day and night. That way, everyone present can be fed by the Word at the same time…Enoch would personally read 40 chapters of the Bible in two hours each day; he would go through the entire Bible in one month, and he did this persistently for two years; so in these two years, he read the entire Bible 24 times.'

The result was that people came to Christ by the hundreds. Naturally, the growth of the church attracted the attention of the police, which caused him to be imprisoned many times.

On one of his early arrests, he was severely beaten, stripped naked and taken outside to be hung upside down in a snowstorm. He was left overnight. Everyone knew he was dead when they went to retrieve his body the next morning.

However, to their surprise, not only was he *not* dead, but his body was also warm and there was no snow beneath where he was hanging.

This infuriated the Chinese police, so they beat him and took him outside again that night. This went on for four nights in a row – they took him outside naked and hung him upside down, only to discover the next morning that he was alive, warm, and well. The prisoners nicknamed him 'Snowman' and this started a house church in the prison as the rest of the prisoners witnessed his faith and wanted to follow Christ as well."

GOD'S UNDERGROUND CHURCH

"Try not to attract too much attention to yourself," my Chinese friends told me as we walked out the front door of the hotel, "and don't talk too much."

I was back in Beijing, which was full of activity at the onset of rush hour traffic. We walked for several blocks without talking then darted into another hotel. After about five minutes, we hurried out the door again and into a taxi. Thirty minutes later, we got out again.

We crossed the street and got into yet another taxi and traveled around the city with no particular destination. After a while, we got out and just stood on the busy street corner for another 15 minutes until a small minivan pulled up. We all piled in.

Our Chinese friends covered us with blankets and told us to lie down and keep out of sight. "Please don't say a word or make a sound," they said. We drove to the outskirts of Beijing and up to the front gate of a Chinese retirement home and quickly pulled the van into the courtyard.

It seemed like "cloak and dagger," but our friends insisted we could not be followed or detected. We were about to find out why.

We quickly ran into the building and were greeted by more than 40 underground Chinese pastors and Christian leaders. Excited to see us, they welcomed us warmly with hugs and huge smiles. We then discovered we would not be allowed to leave the compound for two days.

Millions of Christians in China have refused to register with the government because of all the restrictions. In many places, authorities tell registered pastors what they can and cannot say in their sermons. In other places, they're not allowed to evangelize anyone under the age of 18. Religious freedom is for the "government-sanctioned" churches only — those churches that say and do only what the government allows.

Christians who refuse to register face extreme persecution and are forced to meet secretly underground. In a real sense, they are "God's Underground Church." Because of their stand, they face persecution, arrest, and imprisonment.

And that persecution intensifies with each passing day.

It is true that the Chinese government does permit some churches to meet openly with limited freedoms. These churches are part of the Three Self Patriotic Movement (TSPM). There are many good pastors and believers who are part of the TSPM, but as one pastor recently told me, "God is not the head of the Three-Self Church, the government is."

In a local TSPM church, one of the leaders will normally be politically oriented, responsible for seeing that Communist Party policy is adhered to and that the rules are kept. Bibles are available in limited quantities to the TSPM churches, but only if those who purchase them register their names and addresses.

Almost all the underground leaders we met were severely beaten for their faith and spent time in prison, some for as long as five years. We were humbled to be in their presence.

One group of Chinese brothers and sisters traveled 28 hours one way to meet with us.

We were escorted into a small room and introduced to the leader of one of the largest house-church movements in China. He also was one of the most wanted men in China.

> *"God is not the head of the Three-Self Church, the government is."*

He told us that although it's true that many Chinese own a Bible, he estimated that as many as 80 million Chinese Christians still did not have a copy of God's Word — unbelievable.

This persecuted pastor asked me for 1 million Bibles. Prompted by the Holy Spirit, I said, "yes."

We shook hands and prayed, then he left, not wanting to risk capture in the presence of foreigners.

For the next two days, we sat in a locked room, never leaving the building for security reasons. We couldn't use our real names, and our Chinese friends didn't tell us their real names or where they lived. If we faced interrogation by the police, there would be no way for us to endanger them. They gave me the name Peter.

Paul told me he was the pastor of 20 different house churches in seven separate villages. He was arrested and spent the first four months of his incarceration in handcuffs. He was interrogated every day and beaten; yet he still refused to renounce his faith. Paul spent three years in prison and was forced to perform difficult physical labor, but he still had a smile on his face.

Timothy told me how difficult it was to find Bibles,

so he copied the entire Bible by hand. Caught later by the police, he spent more than five years in prison — his only crime was making a copy of the Bible.

Two of the pastors we met were arrested the day after we left — caught in a Beijing train station while trying to return home.

When I arrived at our hotel after two exhausting days of teaching, praying, and worshipping God, a Chinese worker slipped a piece of paper into my hand. I didn't open it until I reached my room. As I read the handwritten note from our Chinese partner, the regular, ongoing persecution these godly men and women face came into sharp focus.

Dear Peter and other brothers,

Please pray for two pastors who were arrested this morning. Most others who attended the meeting escaped. Some may have problems or are also being arrested, but we don't know yet.

Please pray hard for the two pastors and others who are arrested, that they will be released soon. Others are running. Pray for their safety.

Take care, brothers. This is risky business here in China, but it is worth it to do, even though I might have to give up my life. But God is in control.

Pray ... pray ... pray!

Your brother in Christ,
Barnabas

The next day, we worshipped in a house church of over 2,000 members where more than 90 Chinese crammed into one small room. The 87-year-old pastor sat on the side of his bed in the corner and used the kitchen table as his pulpit. I listened to them pray and worship God in song. The leaders asked me to speak — it was an amazing experience. Twenty of the members also hold house church meetings in their homes.

One woman gave me her personal handwritten Bible and commentary. I didn't want to take it, because I knew the sacrifice she had made to write each verse by hand. But she insisted that I keep it to remember her by. "Let it become a reminder of the urgency to get more Bibles into China," she said.

I didn't know then how we would ever get the resources to print 1 million Bibles. I didn't know how many of our friends would be moved to help us — but God knew.

"Crosses must be removed from all churches because Christianity does not belong in China."[22]

When I returned home, I told our friends these amazing stories and how desperately these believers needed Bibles. But I couldn't tell anyone the details of how we would print and distribute them, because to do so would place our Chinese brothers and sisters in further jeopardy. All I could tell them was that these Bibles would be printed inside China by several different printers in small quantities throughout the country to avoid raising suspicion.

One of my Chinese brothers, John, told me that each Bible provided would touch the lives of 300 people, and on average, 10 Chinese would come to Christ. When Chinese Christians finally receive their own Bibles, they are excited and go door to door, reading Scriptures to all their family and friends. This is how many of the house churches are started.

Every time I visit China, I learn something new. I'm often amazed that well-meaning American Christians say there is religious freedom in China — that persecution no longer exists.

And although there may be many places where this is true, it is not an accurate picture of the entire country. I remember the story of four blind men who each touched an elephant and then tried to describe it. One touched the trunk, one touched the tail, one touched a leg, and the last touched the stomach. Each blind man had a different perspective.

I have heard firsthand about the persecution and suffering from my brothers and sisters in China. I know that persecution still exists there.

According to U.S. government documents, Chinese Christians are being brutally beaten, beheaded, tortured, and some are even crucified. According to the Council on Foreign Relations, China is home to one of the largest populations of religious prisoners, likely numbering in the tens of thousands.

Thousands who escape death are sold into slavery or face long imprisonment. Christian women are raped, children are abused, homes are burned, and forcible abortions are performed — all with the consent or cooperation of the government.

Some dedicated young Christian mothers are even forced to watch their babies starve to death as government officials withhold food — all because these mothers refuse to deny Christ!

The stories of the men and women I have met brought into sharp focus the reality of spiritual warfare and the price dedicated Christians all over China are paying to reach their people for Christ.

Maybe it's because I'm getting older ... or maybe it's because the Lord continues to bring these people into my path ... or maybe it's because of all the horrific stories I hear time and time again ... or maybe it's the personal friendships I am forming with these dear Christians.

But I cannot sit back and say to myself, "I'm tired. God can do this. He doesn't need me. Let someone else do it."

Today in China most Christians ...

- cannot worship at the church of their choice.

- cannot share their faith without government approval.
- cannot print, copy, or distribute Bibles without government permission.
- cannot even accept Bibles from foreign missions organizations like World Help without facing persecution from the government.

We can worship freely ... while many Chinese believers risk their very lives to hear the Word of God preached.

We can share our faith openly ... while many Chinese believers are beaten and thrown in jail for telling others of Christ's love.

THE "HEAVENLY MAN"

Brother Yun, known as China's "Heavenly Man," and three top Christian Chinese leaders were meeting one evening. The police surrounded them and rushed in. Brother Yun turned and ran for a window. He leapt out, only to land in the arms of the many policemen below. He injured both his legs upon landing. They treated him badly during his arrest.

They took all the brothers to one of China's highest security prisons. The police said there was no way that Yun was going to leave this prison alive. To ensure he would never escape, they took him to the torture room upon arriving at the prison. It wasn't enough for them that his legs were already injured. They took a sledgehammer and crushed both legs above the ankle. Only the flesh attached his feet.

Yun was thrown into solitary confinement while the other eight brothers shared a cell. The prison officials told him he was in a special cell because he had escaped so many times. They said it had a steel door and then asked, "Are you still considering escape?"

Despite the unbearable pain from his legs, Yun said, "As soon as the Lord opens the possibility, I will escape." They responded, "There is no way because we are going to keep the door locked 24 hours a day."

There was no toilet in Yun's cell and because he couldn't stand, let alone walk, the prison officials assigned a Christian brother to carry him both down the hall to the toilet and to the torture room in a vain attempt to break him.

God did eventually provide the opportunity for Brother Yun to escape. Yun now reflects on 1 Peter 4:1. *"Therefore, since Christ suffered in his body, arm yourselves also with the same attitude, because he who has suffered in his body is done with sin."*

Yun states, "I believe it is true. In Chinese it says that the one who is suffering is done with sin. I have not yet reached that point because I know when I suffer, I still complain to the Lord. I do believe as suffering increases, sinning

"As soon as the Lord opens the possibility, I will escape."

decreases — but I have not reached that point yet."

He went on to say, "The people who are in prison are not the ones who are suffering, but the ones in the West who are free are the ones who are suffering in a spiritual sense. When people talk to me about what I have experienced in my life, they say, 'You must have had a terrible time when you were in prison.' I respond, 'What are you talking about? I was with Jesus and I had the joy and peace and His very real presence.'

"The real people who suffer are the ones who have never experienced God's presence. One thing is for sure, no matter whether one is from the West or the East, there is a cross that needs to be carried. The cross that God has prepared for the church in the East is persecution, suffering, and loneliness.

"One of the most difficult things Chinese pastors face is when arrested, they don't know how long they will be detained. Maybe the church in the West could not survive these kinds of hardships, but there is a different cross for the church in the West."[23]

CHURCHES, BIBLES DESTROYED

One of the most unsettling reports of persecution made global news in 2019. China destroyed a church that reportedly could seat 3,000 people and detained its pastors under suspicion of "gathering a crowd to disturb social order." The authorities provided no legal documentation to justify the demolition.

Though China's persecution of religious groups has

existed for decades, it has intensified in recent years.

The communist government destroyed or shut down more than 70 Protestant venues — including state-approved Three-Self churches — in 2019, according to persecution watchdog Bitter Winter.

Only **6.8%** of **1.42 billion** Chinese are Christians.

Source: Open Doors

When the True Jesus Church was razed, police officers reportedly dragged Christians out of the building before demolishing the property. Bitter Winter also reported that the Ten Commandments have been removed from numerous Three-Self churches and meeting venues.[24]

The churches that aren't torn down are being turned into factories, cultural centers, and entertainment venues so Christians are unable to meet. This reflects the government's growing concerns about the increasing Christian population of the country.

"The government is eradicating churches," said one pastor.

In addition to pressuring church leaders to include political ideology in their sermons, censors are removing the words "Christ" and "Jesus" from publications and social media networks.[25]

Our partners tell us that Christians have had Bibles confiscated and burned right in front of them and that Christians living in poverty are being told they won't receive any financial assistance if they don't take down their crosses and religious items.

Open Doors ranks China as the 23rd most difficult country for a Christian to live in and it is ranked No. 17 on the watch list for persecution.

And yes, after much hard work and fervent prayer, we were able to provide the 1 million Bibles the church leaders requested. I was reminded once again that where God guides, He provides.

HOW YOU CAN PRAY

We received several requests from pastors in China. One pastor said, "many house churches are forced to split up and revert to 15-20-person cell groups like it was 20-25 years ago." He said this presents many challenges because they need more leaders for individual churches and more Bibles that the different bodies of believers can share.

Another pastor who leads a Bible study and discipleship class said, "My biggest wish is simply for Christians around the world to pray for my students, that they would be willing to suffer for Christ, to be timely servants and soldiers of the Lord, and to win more souls to the Lord."

A third Chinese pastor shared this request: "Please continue to pray for us, that God will grant us strength to hold firm to our faith, never deny Christ, and persevere through our trials. Please pray especially for new believers, as they are still young in their faith and are currently very scared and confused."

FOUR

INDIA

God is Always on Time

2021 WORLD WATCH LIST

Rank: #10
Persecution type: Religious nationalism
Religion: Hinduism
Persecution level: Extreme
Population: 1,383,198,000
Christian: 67,356,000
Government: Federal Parliamentary Republic

Source: Open Doors

INDIA

You will stand trial before governors and kings because you are my followers. But this will be your opportunity to tell the rulers and other unbelievers about me. When you are arrested, don't worry about how to respond or what to say. God will give you the right words at the right time. For it is not you who will be speaking—it will be the Spirit of your Father speaking through you.   — MATTHEW 10:18-20

It was March of 1996 and my first day in India — what an eye-opening experience. By that time, I had already traveled around the world for many years, so I thought I had seen it all. I was no stranger to poverty, filth, and spiritual darkness, but nothing in my travels prepared me for what I experienced in India.

After traveling 38 hours, I arrived in Delhi, a city of over 11 million people. I was overwhelmed by the masses of people everywhere I looked. The poverty, the stench, and the hopelessness on their faces were an all-out assault on my senses.

People were starving as "sacred" cows walked down the streets. Children roamed about with little, if any, clothing. People slept in cardboard boxes, and filthy sewage filled the streets. I saw the worst traffic and driving conditions imaginable, pollution, trash everywhere, and an unmistakable sense of spiritual oppression. I was in culture shock.

I wasn't sure why God had sent me to India, but He sure had my attention.

We took a seven-hour train ride from Delhi to a remote part of Rajasthan, home to the Maharajas. At the train station, there were thousands of people — diseased, blind, crippled, poor, and destitute — it was overwhelming. Before I left the U.S. I had asked God to break my heart with the things that break His heart — and He certainly did.

I took a few minutes to catch my breath, then we were off again for a bumpy six-hour ride in an old jeep. When we finally reached our destination, I was exhausted and totally out of my comfort zone but excited about what God was going to do.

The next morning, our small team drove about an hour out of town to the remote village of Karpina. I was told there wasn't a church within 50 miles in any direction. I met a young pastor who had discipled 192 new believers in only 14 months. They were meeting together under a tree; they didn't have a church building.

That's why we were there.

We dedicated an unfinished building provided by a group of Liberty University students. It was only 9 a.m., yet more than 200 people had already arrived to witness this unusual event. Some walked as far as 20 miles one way to attend. The pastor had no car — not even a bicycle — yet he had already accomplished so much.

Another young pastor told me, "We have a thousand pastors trained and ready right now to plant a thousand new churches. All we need is some help."

It was then I heard the still small voice of God saying, "Vernon, this why I brought you to India. This is why I spared your life from cancer and gave you a new lease on life. This is why World Help was started. This is what I want you to do for the rest of your life — help plant churches where no churches exist."

I quickly did the math in my mind — $4,000 to build one church building multiplied by 1,000 trained pastors — that's $4 MILLION!

I prayed silently, "God, I can't do this. It's too big!" And once again I heard that small voice of God say, "Good ... I can!"

I soon discovered there were over 500,000 villages in India, and the majority didn't have a church of any kind. God's vision for me was clear — 1,000 new churches. To make sure I would follow through, I set a deadline to complete the vision by the year 2000. That very day, *Vision 1000* was born.

I returned home so excited. When I told my family and friends what I had experienced and my vision to see 1,000 new churches planted and 1,000 new buildings built by the year 2,000, some of them laughed.

John Maxwell once told me, "Vernon, if you tell someone your vision and they don't laugh, it's not big enough."

One of my board members tried to bring me back to my

> *God give me a servant's heart … allow me to display humility. God fill me with your Holy Spirit, use me for Your purposes. I want to be a man of prayer. Little prayer … little power, more prayer… more power, much prayer … much power.* — V.B.

senses by suggesting I lower the goal to 200 churches, but it didn't work. My vision from God was clear — crystal clear!

My wife, Patty, and I knew if I was going to spend the next few years asking people to help make this vision a reality, we needed to provide the first church ourselves. I had just purchased a really nice, used car, but we decided to sell it. We drove an older car for over a year — but it sure was worth it.

The funds we sent to India were used to build a church building in a city of at least 200,000 people. It was the only church in the entire city. We decided to dedicate it in honor of my parents, Fred and Vivian Brewer, for their more than 50 years of dedicated service to the ministry.

They were incredibly happy. I even helped them raise the funds to go to India for the dedication — it was quite the event. More than 1,000 people showed up. Even local and state government officials were there. They had never experienced a church building dedication, so they thought they were just supposed to be there.

At the last minute, I was asked to speak. I shared a simple message about God's love and explained that Jesus Christ died and rose from the dead. Many Hindu men and women became Christ-followers that night.

I will never forget the look of joy on my parents' faces as they saw the vision God had so clearly given me begin to become a reality.

A few months later, l was back in India. The pastor of the church we helped build identified 20 villages surrounding his city, established house churches in each village, and already had more than 300 baptized believers.

One by one, God brought people across my path to make the vision possible. I soon learned that when the vision is God's — He will make it happen. Churches caught the vision. Friends, family members, and people I didn't even know wanted to be part of something bigger than themselves.

John Maxwell once told me, "Vernon, if you tell someone your vision and they don't laugh, it's not big enough."

A year later, my wife's father died. He was one of the finest Christian men I knew. One day, not long after the funeral, while I prepared to leave for a trip, Patty sat on the steps and began to cry. I thought she was sad because I was leaving. But instead, she said, "I miss my dad. Could we build another church in India," she asked, "this time in memory of him?"

Our gift went to the city of Alwar, and a new church building was built where no church existed. But at the time, we didn't realize the significance of Alwar.

Alwar is not the best place to start a new church. In fact, the name Alwar means "the city which housed the throne of Satan." It was a strong anti-Christian city.

Many years ago, an evangelist named Dori Raj went to Alwar to start a church. The militant Hindus said, "If you don't leave, we will kill you." Dori Raj replied, "God has called me here, and I will not leave."

They did kill Dori Raj and his body was never found. At his memorial service, his 8-year-old nephew Solomon stood up to address the crowd.

"Someday I will go to work for Christ in Alwar where my uncle died," he said, "and I will die also, if necessary." When Solomon grew up, he went away to Bible college. After he graduated, he did as he promised and went to Alwar to start a church. He used the money we sent to build a church building.

On the walls of the churches in India, you will find a Martyr's Board. It lists the names of the men and women who have paid the ultimate price for their faith and the date they went to be with the Lord.

In a baptismal service at one of these churches, I witnessed 59 people coming for baptism. They were asked three questions: Will you live for Jesus Christ? Will you obey Jesus Christ? And if necessary, will you die for Jesus Christ?

In fact, John Maxwell and I were in India training pastors and church planters when over 1,000 men and women stood and made this pledge, to die for Jesus Christ.

Can you imagine the level of commitment that would be required of Western Christians if these same questions were asked of us? Would we be willing to answer, yes?

My family was privileged to be in Alwar to dedicate that new church building with Solomon. Somehow, I knew that looking down from heaven were at least two very happy men — Dori Raj, the martyred pastor; and Glen Bentley, my wife's father, a coal miner from West Virginia.

For several years, I cast this vision everywhere I went, and people caught it.

On December 31, 1999, we were still 10 churches away from reaching our goal. I was home when the phone rang. Someone I didn't even know called to tell me he was mailing a check for $40,000 to build 10 new churches. I looked at my watch. It was 1:27 in the afternoon. We did it with plenty of time to spare.

I have always said, "God is seldom early, but never late." This time, He was early.

But, as I watched the news bring in the new millennium around the world, I realized that with the unusual 10-and-a-half-hour time difference in India, it was actually midnight in New Delhi. And then it hit me. God did it — He did it on India time.[26]

Hindu extremists believe all Indians should be Hindus, and the country should be rid of Christianity and Islam. Radical Hindus view Christians as blemishes to be removed, and a hostile atmosphere makes it difficult for believers to share their faith.

Only **4.9** percent of India's population is Christian.

Source: Open Doors

THEY ALL SAID THEY'D GO BACK

I met some Indian Bible college students who were asked if they would like to go into an unreached village where there was no church or Christian witness of any kind. In fact, no Christians had ever gone into this village to minister and come back alive.

When they arrived at the village, they began witnessing and distributing Bibles and Gospel tracts. The militant Hindus, who are very anti-Christian, immediately turned on them and began to hit them ... all 79 were severely beaten.

One young man was tied to a tree with a cloth coat hanger stuffed down his throat to keep him from sharing the Gospel. Several of the female students were molested. One young student was held down while his hands were beaten with a metal pipe for distributing Bibles.

The students were threatened with death and told to leave and never return. The militants poured kerosene on their bus and tried to set it on fire as they drove away. They narrowly escaped with their lives.

As they wiped the blood from their faces, the students began to weep. Not because of their own pain and suffering, but because they were brokenhearted over the many people in that village who had never heard of Jesus Christ.

When they were asked how many would be willing to go back to that village again … all 79 said they would return.

I wonder how many of us in America would be willing to sacrifice our own lives for that village?

HE WOULDN'T WORSHIP AN IDOL

A Hindu priest, who had just recently become a Christ follower, was kidnapped by a group of anti-Christians. They made him walk around the Hindu temple 25 times, filled his mouth with urine mixed with alcohol, and forced him to swallow.

They tried to make him worship an idol, but he told them, "I was the one waking early and ringing the bell. I worshipped this stone, washed it, cleaned it, and kept it painted for many years, but it never helped me, changed me, nor gave me peace and joy. Now that I worship the living God — death is not a threat to me because I will be with my God in heaven."

The anti-Christians released him after a few hours. There is now a growing church in that area.

HOW YOU CAN PRAY

Many people face persecution from their own family members if they convert from Hinduism. That's what happened to one young man who made this request: "Please pray for my protection. If my family finds me, they will certainly kill me because of my faith in Christ." This young man had to flee his own home to follow Jesus, but he's refusing to turn his back on God and is sharing the Gospel in his new community.

Pray for protection, especially for new Christians and those living in areas that are particularly isolated. Ask God to help their families and communities accept their new faith.

Another man in South Asia asked: "Kindly pray for my family as we receive threats from people." Ever since his family became Christians, they have been constantly harassed by their neighbors, especially his young daughter. And while they ask for protection, not a single member of the family has ever wavered in their faith.

FROM MY PRAYER JOURNAL

Today, I leave India with a bit of sadness ... but somehow, I know I will be back. There are many experiences and many images burned into my heart and mind — forever!

I will never forget the graduation service where the students were asked to stand if they were willing to die for Christ. Every student stood — they were committed to die, if necessary, to carry the Gospel to their nation of India. I will never forget their commitment.

I will never forget one pastor saying, "I would have no greater joy than to die a martyr's death for my Lord Jesus Christ.

I pray that might be my privilege someday." He meant every word! He continued, "I have one son. I hope he outlives me by many years. But I would be glad for him to die a martyr's death for our Lord." He was crying ... so was I.

I will never forget the faces of those 1,000 pastors and students as we taught them God's Word — they are the hope for the future.

I will never forget the little leper girl whose arms and legs were twisted and deformed or the sight of people bowing down and worshipping idols on the side of the road.

I will never be able to forget the look of hopelessness, so abundant in the eyes of the children. I must let God use me to make a difference here.

Lord, don't let me avoid persecution. Take my eyes off fame, power, prestige. God, don't let me quit. Change the way I live, the way I view life, the way I spend money. Let me live more with you in focus.

Thank you for breaking my heart! Please don't ever let me be the same again!

FIVE

VIETNAM

God's Silent Church

2021 WORLD WATCH LIST

Rank: #19
Persecution type: Communist and post-communist oppression
Religion: Buddhism
Persecution level: Very high
Population: 98,360,000
Christian: 8,924,000
Government: Communist state

Source: Open Doors

VIETNAM

We are pressed on every side by troubles, but we are not crushed. We are perplexed, but not driven to despair. We are hunted down, but never abandoned by God. We get knocked down, but we are not destroyed. Through suffering, our bodies continue to share in the death of Jesus so that the life of Jesus may also be seen in our bodies.

— 2 CORINTHIANS 4:8-10

"You must do *exactly* what you're told if you want to protect these pastors and churches."

I was already anxious and excited about my first visit to Vietnam several years ago. I was to secretly meet with 52 pastors, church planters, and evangelists and had been told the security would be extremely tight. But when I received the warning above, it brought home the reality of just how dangerous it was for these men and women to meet with a fellow believer.

It reminded me of my first Romanian experience before the fall of communism, and I felt as if I had stepped back into the past. However, nothing prepared me for the people I would meet and the intensive and heartbreaking stories I would hear during the next three days.

The following are excerpts from my journal.

DAY ONE: A SURREAL EXPERIENCE

As we landed in Ho Chi Minh City, I didn't quite know what to expect. At the airport we saw visible reminders of a war from decades earlier. Most Vietnamese weren't even born in 1965 when the U.S. began to send troops ... all they know is communism.

No photos were allowed at the airport, but the sight was unforgettable. It was hot and humid and a mass of people ... palm trees in the distance. I felt like if I closed my eyes, I would hear the roar of helicopter blades and see young American soldiers preparing to die. It was all too surreal for me. It is the Lunar New Year (TET) this week so there are lots of celebrations.

Within a few hours of arriving, we were taken to a special place and met with 27 men and women who were pastors, evangelists, and church planters. They were introduced to us as our "friends." We could not call them pastors ... could not mention God ... could not bow our heads ... could not open our Bibles.

We could not use their real names or tell what area they were working in because to do so would put them in danger. We were asked not to take any photographs of our "friends" ... and as they began to speak, we found out the reasons why.

The first person to share was a man pastoring among the tribal areas. Three years ago, when he went there, there were only four Christians. When we met, he had six churches with 28 believers. The government will not give him land for a house to meet in and will not allow the children of the Christians to attend school.

The next pastor also was working in unreached tribal areas. Five years ago, he had only one church with 60 believers. He shared that he now has more than 45 churches with 3,360 Christians.

Vietnam's beautiful countryside of rice paddies, mountains, and rural villages stretch for over 1,000 miles along the South China Sea. But Vietnam has not always experienced serene beauty; war has marred the landscape and foreign powers have ruthlessly dominated Vietnam for over 1,000 years.

First China, then France, and finally the United States sent their young men to fight and die in the steamy jungles and mountain passes of this rugged land. Vietnam's independence came when Communist guerillas under the leadership of Ho Chi Minh finally wrested control of both the northern and southern halves of the country.

The Buddhist religion practiced by the majority of the Vietnamese people is a blend of Confucianism, Taoism, and Buddhism, with popular Chinese beliefs and ancient

Vietnamese animism mixed in. This mixture of ancestor and spirit worship is known as Tam Giao. Though the Gospel has been widely proclaimed in Vietnam, the hill tribes are isolated from these efforts to proclaim the good news.

It was not until the 20th century that Protestant missionaries gained a permanent foothold in Vietnam, and even then, the work was conducted largely by one mission, the Christian and Missionary Alliance. From the outset, those serving in Vietnam have suffered persecution. Though the nationals were normally open to the Gospel, it was the ruling powers that felt threatened. During the French colonial period, evangelistic work was severely curtailed, and when the Japanese moved in during World War II, the missionaries who refused to leave were held in internment camps.

It is said that the church is born in the blood of the martyrs, and that is certainly true of Vietnam.[27]

He has been arrested many times — once spending nine months in prison and fined two months' salary for evangelizing. Many of the children who accept Christ are beaten by their parents. But after they see the change in their children, many of the parents come to Christ, as well.

> *Dear God, how fortunate I am to live in a free country, where there is no persecution, where I can worship at the church of my choice, where I am FREE to serve my Lord and Savior. I am so very fortunate! God, what do you want me to do?. — V.B.*

Another pastor has nine churches and over 500 believers. He has been fined and persecuted many times. He said it so matter of fact ... it is a way of life for him. He told how three police accepted Christ because of the believers' testimonies.

The next pastor from the Mekong Delta region told how a lieutenant colonel in the army came into his church to tear it down. He put his hands on a chair to throw it out and started shaking so much he couldn't move. He ran out afraid. The next day he came back and said, "You are worshipping the true God. I will leave you alone."

One of the foremost Christian leaders in the entire country was with us and I didn't even realize it. He is responsible for overseeing more than 1,000 churches. He told about a pastor working in one of the remote tribal areas. The police came with pre-printed forms stating, "I will forsake Christianity and re-establish my ancestral family altar." They threatened to kill all 430 Christians in that village if they didn't sign the statement. Because they were afraid, they signed the document but immediately fled the area.

All 40 families packed up what few belongings they had and traveled over 1,000 miles to a remote region in the mountains and re-established their homes there. They have now established several house churches. When one of the Christian friends found out where they had moved, he asked them, "How do you feel?" They said, "Great! Now we have freedom to worship."

As I heard this dedicated Christian leader share this testimony, it reminded me of what it was like for Christians in the book of Acts.

This wonderful Christian leader had spent seven years in prison because another pastor had been an informant and turned him in. I can't begin to imagine what it must be like to live in an atmosphere of fear and distrust.

The next pastor shared how the secret police were beating the Christian children in his village — severely! The children prayed for the persecution to stop and that night a snake came out of the forest and bit the policeman ... the next day he died! The entire village realized the power of God!

What an incredible day this has been. For four hours we listened to these Giants of God share what God was doing. *God, I feel so ashamed, so humbled.*

Meeting with the first of the 52 pastors was an incredible experience. My heart was broken — my resolve to do ministry in this country was more than just an idea, it laid on my heart like a ton of bricks. These pastors and Christian leaders desperately need our help.

DAY TWO: A SMILE ON THEIR FACE

Today, nine more "friends" met with us.

Another 44-year-old pastor had a broken skull and 12 bullets in his body from the Cambodian War. The police arrested him and tortured him by hanging him upside down. He started bleeding from his mouth and nose.

The next pastor was 50 years old and had served as an officer for the Viet Cong in the Vietnam War. After the war, he became an alcoholic and was very dissatisfied with life. He heard the Gospel for the first time, and he, his wife, and four children all knelt and received Christ. Since then, he has personally started 93 new churches and has trained 45 church planters who are working in the north.

A 20-year-old pastor told us that when he was 6 years old, he ran away from home because his father brought his mistress into the house and there was fighting every day — he was physically abused. He ran to the country and kept water buffalo for a family. When he was 18, he heard the Gospel and accepted Christ. He returned to his home, but they were so angry that he had become a Christian, they beat him and wouldn't let him live at home.

The church took him in and taught him. Now he is a young pastor in the same area where he used to keep the water buffalo. However, he still faces severe persecution. The police beat him regularly for preaching the Gospel. He has been arrested many times. Once they kept him four days without food and water. They confiscated his Bible, books, and bicycle. He had to walk nearly 100 miles to get back to the city.

We prayed for all these pastors and felt so unworthy to even be in their presence. Every one of them had a smile on their face and the joy of the Lord in their heart.

That night we had dinner in a remote restaurant. We were joined by Pastor James and six of his pastors. He oversees 915 churches and 80,000 believers. He is the leading Christian leader in Vietnam. He spent 26 months in prison. He told me, "We are the silent church." They have already reached 24 of the 53 unreached ethnic tribes of Vietnam.

He has 8,000 new church planters being trained with 42 trainers who go into the districts and provide the teaching and resources to train them. Pastor James told me that they train them in three areas: the Heart ... the Head ... and the Hand (spiritual life, theology, and evangelism). He stressed that there must be a balance of all three. They saw 45,000 new converts last year alone — incredible!

They require a three-month doctrine class before they will baptize a new believer. They also have an extensive children's ministry and when the non-believing parents see the change in their children, they soon become Christians, also. Pastor James told me, "Persecution creates examples of faith — it trains our people to stay strong."

These past two days have been incredible as we spent over nine hours meeting with these godly men and women who pay a great price for their faith. The story of "God's Silent Church" must be told.

> Lord, you've made yourself very clear. I know in my heart what I must do. I know I can't do it all ... but I can do something. — V.B.

DAY THREE: "I WILL STAND FOR JESUS CHRIST"

Today, we traveled five hours to a remote area, where three churches had been torn down by the communists. We were going to meet with the pastors to encourage them.

We arrived at a remote tribal village of thatched houses where we met with 10 pastors. They told us how the communist authorities had destroyed three of their church buildings. Not long after that, these authorities lost their jobs and are now working in the rice fields. One of the pastors has been planting churches for the past seven years since he was 17. Today, he has 50 churches with more than 7,000 believers.

For security reasons, we could only stay for 15 minutes. We did not want an informant to see us and turn these pastors in to the authorities. We drove five hours to meet with them for 15 minutes. But their smiles and handshakes told us we had really encouraged them in their ministry.

We knelt and prayed with these faithful servants, realizing they would probably be arrested and beaten because of our presence.

After we prayed, I met with one of the pastors privately and told him we would help him rebuild those three churches, plus provide the funds and materials for the two more they need. He was overjoyed!

When he was 16 years old, an evangelist came to his village and presented the Gospel. He asked if there was anyone there who would stand up for Jesus Christ. No one moved. Finally, this young man stood and said, "I will stand for Jesus Christ." Soon he led his friend to Christ, and they went into the jungle and built a prayer house where they prayed every day. Soon the Gospel spread and now there are thousands of believers because of this young man's stand for Jesus Christ.

On the way back, we drove through a remote village with 450 believers. All but two of the families are Christians — the other two are Communist party members. For security reasons, we did not get out of the van but just smiled and waved as many believers came out to greet us. It was unbelievable to see an entire unreached village come to Christ.

In just three days, I had the incredible opportunity to talk with 52 of the most courageous and committed pastors, evangelists, and church planters I think I have ever met. What an incredible experience!

Lord, how can we not do something ... anything? This is not only an incredible opportunity, this is also a tremendous responsibility! — V.B.

"WE STAY IN A CAVE"

Another Vietnamese evangelist shared this firsthand account of persecution:

I was arrested December 29 in our village. The police came and handcuffed me and another brother and said, "You illegally proclaim the Gospel." Our wives and children began to cry. At the station we were told, "You will not leave prison until Jesus comes back to earth!"

I was sent to a brick labor camp where 24 prisoners were held. I was the only Christian. Then I was transferred to another camp where I drank water from a pond and was given two bowls of rice a day. Our quota was to walk 100 meters carrying 2,200 bricks per day. My body weight dropped from 105 to 95 pounds. The guards hit me with steel construction rods to get me to move faster.

I worked seven days a week. At night I lay on the bed. I was so tired from the brickwork. I was too tired to remember many Bible verses, but I prayed, and God was there.

After I was released from the camp with the other Christian brother, we went back to our village. The police came and told us, "If you do not leave Jesus and put a worship altar for spirits back in your house, we will take you to prison again."

We refused to do this. Now in the daytime we stay in a cave, and at night we travel down to the village to be with our families. Our children are strong Christians. One is an evangelist. They all share their faith.

We were told by another Hmong Christian who had worked in the brick camps, "The police tell us, 'You cannot have Hmong Bibles, because you are supposed to read Vietnamese.' Then we ask for a Vietnamese Bible, they tell us, 'No, you cannot have a Vietnamese Bible, because you are Hmong!'" They meet us when we get off the buses to go back up into the hills. They check our bags for Bibles. If they find one, they take it from us and beat us."[28]

HOW YOU CAN PRAY

Ask God to raise up a vast army of workers to go throughout Vietnam and plant churches.

Communism is one more form of oppression. Ask the Lord for a revival to sweep this land – not only for the people, but for the government leaders, as well.

Pray for believers who gather to worship each Sunday, that God would strengthen them, give them boldness, and take away fear and hurt.

Intercede for spiritual awakening among all those who profess the name of Jesus in Vietnam.

FROM MY PRAYER JOURNAL

Oh, God, you've touched my heart as only you can. Thank you! I must help these pastors, evangelists, and church plants who are sacrificing so much to reach their country for Christ. I know that I cannot go home without doing everything in my power to help these men and women of God.

God, you brought me to this place, at this time, to help these people. Thank you for your love for the people of Vietnam and for your wisdom and guidance in bringing World Help to this country. Help us not to close our eyes ... but to open our hearts to this great need!

I know you already have people waiting back home for this opportunity ... to do something that will outlive them and last for eternity!

Thank you for showing me the thousands of persecuted Christians who suffer every day for the cause of Christ.

Thank you for refocusing my attention on what is really important in this life and what really matters.

Thank you for allowing me to be in the presence of your humble servants who have been beaten, tortured, arrested, humiliated, and ridiculed. Never let me ever complain again ... as long as I live.

Thank you for showing me how we can help them. Please don't let me close my eyes to this great opportunity ... but open my heart to what you want me to do.

Thank you, Lord, for prolonging my life ... for healing me from cancer ... for allowing me to serve you.

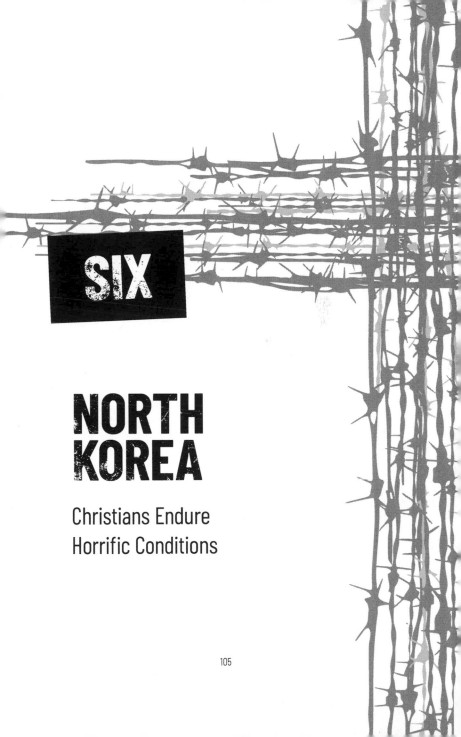

SIX

NORTH KOREA

Christians Endure
Horrific Conditions

2021 WORLD WATCH LIST

Rank: #1
Persecution type: Communist and post-communist oppression
Religion: Agnosticism
Persecution level: Extreme
Population: 25,841,000
Christian: 400,000
Government: Single-party dictatorship

Source: Open Doors

NORTH KOREA

Remember those in prison, as if you were there yourself. Remember also those being mistreated, as if you felt their pain in your own bodies.   — HEBREWS 13:3

For twenty consecutive years, Open Doors has ranked North Korea "the most oppressive place in the world for Christians."[29]

Often sick and malnourished, these captives are subjected to extreme violence and crude torture, suffering beatings with electric rods and metal poles and even being used as test subjects for medical experiments, as reported in Christian Solidarity Worldwide's 2016 report on North Korea.

A 15-year sentence for being caught with a Bible, praying, or singing a hymn is actually a death sentence since most Christians survive only a few years in these brutal camps.

Nearly 20 percent of the country's Christians — between 50,000 to 70,000 — are currently imprisoned in labor camps. There are believed to be approximately 400,000 Christians living in this nation where the persecution level is rated as "extreme."

Life in the camps is unbearable.

I will never forget my first day in North Korea. As we

drove over the Tumen River, our guide told us how North Koreans come to the riverbank and wait until evening to attempt the risky swim to Mainland China.

The border guards have orders to shoot on sight and anyone attempting to cross the border illegally is subject to summary execution. Our guide then added, almost as an afterthought, "The Tumen has probably witnessed more deaths than any other river in the world."

Once inside the country, I was suddenly struck by the eerie quietness that pervades the towns and cities we visited. The streets were empty, absent of the usual traffic, and busy city life and the few people who found themselves outside seemed to meander aimlessly.

Convoys of ox carts replaced cars and public buses, and the buildings with their water-stained stucco walls looked hollow and gray. Electricity was often cut off so that at night entire towns were absorbed into darkness.

I was shocked to see students typing on keyboards while staring at blank computer screens at one government school. They were pretending to do their classwork until the power came back on.

The Democratic People's Republic of Korea—a communist state of 25 million souls—is considered the most secretive nation on earth. Driven by the Kim family into isolation and a cultic reverence to the royal family, this small nation now threatens to destabilize the world with nuclear warfare. Religious persecution is the world's greatest and most enduring crisis.

Many people don't remember that in the early 20th

century, Pyongyang was known as "the Jerusalem of the East" or that Christianity played a main role in the history of the Korean peninsula. Even after communism began to overtake North Korea, Christianity's influence was so prevalent that Kim Il Sung's father was a Christian and his father-in-law was a Presbyterian minister.

Nowhere is persecution of believers more severe than in North Korea. I am not even able to share with you many of the atrocities committed against these believers—especially the stories of how hundreds of Christ followers are executed every year.

In one instance, when a group of church leaders did not reject Christ, police directed that a bulldozer be driven over them, crushing them to death.

TORTURE ALMOST BREAKS HIS SPIRIT

For my good friend and ministry partner Charlie, what he endured in prison brought him to the edge of despair. The treatment he received was so harsh, the pain he experienced so severe, he actually contemplated suicide.

Charlie directed our North Korea Bible distribution program and made many secret trips into the country to make sure the Bibles get into the hands of the right people. It was on one of those trips that Charlie was arrested.

He was charged with espionage, he endured daily interrogations, frequent and severe beatings, and suffered intense physical and psychological torture. His actual "crime?" Being a committed follower of Christ.

The determination of North Korean officials to break

Charlie's spirit and get him to deny his faith was intense. Even a personal visit and plea by former President Jimmy Carter to gain his release was unsuccessful.

Finally, after eight months of torture, Charlie was released, but his health was extremely poor and his spirit low.

While he now appears to be doing well, he has lost a tremendous amount of weight. Doctors are closely watching for any signs of Post-Traumatic Stress Disorder (PTSD). Please pray for a rapid recovery — physically, mentally, and emotionally.

Amazingly, Charlie's horrific experiences have not lessened his commitment to share his faith. His desire to deliver Bibles into North Korea and to train underground church leaders remains strong.

ENDURING UNIMAGINABLE CRUELTY

One of our partners working in North Korea told me a heartbreaking account of 81 believers who survived the horrors of prison camp. The descriptions I heard were staggering, gut-wrenching . . . enough to steal your breath away.

All prisoners were forced to perform 12 hours or more of intense slave labor a day, from the smallest child to the physically disabled — even pregnant women. With each description, my friend's voice grew more solemn.

He told me of believers being beaten mercilessly by prison guards. Entire families tortured physically and psychologically. Young men mutilated and dismembered.

Small girls made to endure sexual humiliation and torment. Pregnant woman forced to carry heavy rocks until they miscarried their unborn children. Cruelty so intense that I cannot even share all the details with you.

This is what our North Korean brothers and sisters face simply for identifying themselves as Christians . . . and yet they refuse to deny Christ! In the face of inconceivable evil, they choose to love. Even as they watch their loved ones — even their children — being tortured, they still proclaim that God is good!

Put yourself in their place — can you imagine losing everything for the sake of Christ?

THE COST OF A RED SCARF

"There was one homework [assignment] I wish I'd never done," said Eun, now in her 40s.

One morning, when Eun was in third grade, her teacher told the class, "Today we're not going to give you homework." Naturally, all the children celebrated the news, but the teacher wasn't finished.

"However, when you go home, look for a book," the teacher continued. "Normally it's black. Normally it's hidden. Normally it's the book your mom or dad read when you sleep. Normally it's hidden in the closet or the drawer or somewhere that's not reachable, but if you look hard enough you can find this book.

"And, if you bring it, we will honor you."

Eun ran home, arriving before her mom. She looked everywhere, through drawers, cabinets, underneath mattresses, until she finally found a small, black, leather-bound book. She hid it inside her bag and took it to school the next morning.

At school, Eun's teacher gave her a red scarf — the sign of a good kid in communist North Korea. Eun's mother didn't allow her to be involved in government-sponsored extracurricular activities, so Eun had never had the opportunity to receive this honor.

With the scarf around her neck, she ran home to tell her mom what had happened — but her mom wasn't there. In fact, Eun waited all night for her mom, but she never arrived.

When Eun got to school the following day, with an empty stomach, she found out the parents of 14 other students also hadn't come home the night before.

But the persecution in North Korea is not just something that occurred when Eun was a little girl some 30 years ago. It is even worse today.

WITNESS TO HIS TORTURERS

When I traveled to the North Korean border for the first time, many expressed concerns for my safety. After all, the country has been shrouded in secrecy for many years. But one thing that isn't a secret is that North Korea is consistently ranked the worst place in the world for Christians to live.

I heard the story of one 17-year-old boy who escaped North Korea and was working in China when God called him to go back home and share the Gospel.

He decided the best way he could help others was by

delivering copies of God's Word.

On his way into the country, soldiers stopped and searched him. When they found the Bibles, they began beating him. The boy cried out, not pleading with them to stop, but pleading with them to believe in Jesus.

Each time he said the name "Jesus," the guards hit him harder. But he continued to witness to his torturers. Finally, one of the guards asked him why this Jesus was worth dying for. The boy explained the Gospel to him, and that soldier accepted Christ.

The boy was eventually sentenced to a firing squad, but he said that his life was full because God had used him to lead someone to Christ.

"DO YOU BELIEVE IN JESUS?"

Deep in a secluded area, the men dug several shallow graves before ordering the family to get in. With each shovel of fresh dirt, the father and his six children's screams grew softer until the forest was silent.

Jun grew up hearing the story of how his great-grandfather was buried alive.

The situation in North Korea hasn't changed much since the 1940s, Jun said, when his great-grandfather was a pastor living in North Korea. Jun is now a pastor himself.

Jun's great-grandfather, Hoon, moved to North Korea to escape Christian persecution in China. Six of his children accompanied him while his wife and one daughter stayed behind, planning to join them soon.

But Hoon's wife and daughter would never see their

family members alive again.

As Hoon and the children settled into their new home, he thought he'd finally be able to spread the Gospel in freedom. But North Korea was becoming more closed, and the government was beginning to seek out Christians, imprison them — and even kill them.

One day as Hoon's youngest daughter was playing in the yard, she was approached by a neighbor. "Do you believe in Jesus?" he asked her.

"Yes," she said.

A North Korean communist overheard the conversation, and later that day, men burst into Hoon's home and dragged him and his children away.

When Hoon's wife finally arrived in North Korea, the government contacted her and told her where she could find her husband.

As the dirt was brushed away from her family's lifeless bodies, Hoon's wife realized her husband died with his arms spread out, trying to protect and comfort his youngest daughter as they died.

Now, 70 years later, Jun is carrying on his great-grandfather's legacy. He refuses to let what happened to his family in North Korea hinder him from serving the Lord. He's dedicated his life to ministering to the persecuted Christians living there.

"I had decided that I would not look at the land of North Korea after I heard that story from my grandmother," Jun said. "But now I am doing it because God has given me love for North Korea. The situation in North Korea in these days is no different from that period. Let us pray for the soul of North Korea and for the freedom of faith."

"North Korean people are so cut off and disconnected from the outside world that they don't even know what the word 'internet' means." — Kim Min Hyuk, escaped in 2006

"I'LL BE BACK TOMORROW"

Jang-mi was startled as the door to her cell swung open. Bruised, bloody, and soaked from her captives' attempts to wake her with buckets of water, she was surprised to see her uncle walk through the door.

Just two months earlier, Jang-mi was happily married and living in China. She had successfully escaped North Korea and was living in a Chinese border town where she met and fell in love with her husband, who also was from North Korea. It wasn't long before they discovered freedom of a different kind — they were introduced to Jesus.

With a heart on fire for Christ, Jang-mi's husband told her he had decided to return to North Korea to share the Gospel with his family and friends.

"I'll be back tomorrow," he told her.

She watched as he crossed the frozen river, headed back into North Korea. She hoped and prayed his final words would be true. Surely, she would see him tomorrow.

But she didn't.

A few days went by, then a week, then a month. Worried, Jang-mi decided she couldn't wait any longer — she had to go look for her husband. Crossing the North Korean and Chinese border would be dangerous. North Korean police are instructed to shoot on sight.

Jang-mi mustered her courage and quietly attempted to cross the border. Almost immediately, she was captured and thrown into prison.

All day and all night, Jang-mi endured torture. It only worsened when her captors found out she was a Christian. The soldiers yelled at her, calling her — ironically — "Judas" for betraying North Korea.

Through it all, Jang-mi remained strong. She even began to share her faith with her torturers.

Finally, Jang-mi was released, and her uncle brought her to her family home. There, he gave her a gift — her father's old military hat.

"Your father wanted you to have this," he said. "Look inside the hat."

Jang-mi looked inside the cap and tugged on the interior flap. There, in the place where most soldiers wrote their names, was a little cross. Jang-mi was shocked.

"You mean my father was a believer in Jesus?" Jang-mi asked. "But how? Why did he never tell me?"

"Because he was trying to protect you and your family," her uncle replied.

When a Christian is discovered sharing the Gospel or

holding a single page of God's Word, they can be sentenced to 15 years in a harsh labor camp. Few people come out alive.

Jang-mi's father is now in one of those prison camps. She knows he probably won't outlive his sentence. She also found out that her husband had been caught crossing the border and was later executed for his faith.

Heartbroken, Jang-mi once more risked the cold crossing back into China. She saw her old friends, stayed in her old home, and she remembered once more how passionate her husband had been about sharing the Gospel. She thought about her father, and how he, too, was willing to die for his faith.

"I have to go back," she thought. "I have to go back and tell those who have not heard."

THE GOSPEL ON A TRAIN SEAT

Sung-Min tried — and failed — to escape North Korea four separate times. Each time, he was caught and sent back home. He spent many years doing hard labor in North Korea's prison camps. But Sung-Min never gave up hope that someday he would be free.

I met Sung-Min during my last visit to the North Korean border. I remember his face, and the stories he told me stick with me even now.

He said he believed freedom was worth any cost. Sung-Min's father had always dreamed of taking his family to China or South Korea. He hated raising his children in a country where they could be thrown in labor camps for breaking even the smallest rule. He longed for a life free from the fear of oppression. But he died before he and his family could escape.

Sung-Min wanted to fulfill his father's dream, so he tried to flee the country in secret. He didn't know that soon he would discover the only *true* source of freedom — Jesus.

During his second escape attempt, Sung-Min met a group of Christians who introduced him to the Gospel. Although he was eventually captured again, he brought his newfound faith with him to his prison cell and labor camp in North Korea.

Life in the labor camps is worse than you and I could ever imagine. Believers are beaten and abused for hours on end. Still, Sung-Min and many just like him are able to withstand the torture and remain steadfast in their faith.

One day after his release from prison, Sung-Min discovered a Bible lying on a train seat. The Bible had been smuggled into the country by some of our partners. Sung-Min was so excited he had found it! He knew several security guards were watching him. So instead of taking the whole Bible, Sung-Min ripped out a single page from the book of Matthew.

He read that page over and over, committing it to memory. When he was thrown into jail after another escape attempt, the verses brought him comfort and hope. And it didn't just affect him.

Sung-Min passed the page of Matthew on to his sister, and now she is a Christian, too. Later, he discovered that both his mother and grandmother were also secret believers. His grandmother was even a deaconess in the underground church — but she had never seen a Bible. She had heard about people owning one, but she had never held the Scriptures in her own hands.

On his fifth attempt to escape, Sung-Min finally made it. Today he prays that more copies of the Word of God will reach his nation.

HOW YOU CAN PRAY

Pray for the underground churches of North Korea. Several thousand secret churches meet in homes, caves, forests, and shores ... and need our prayers.

Pray that believers will continue to boldly share their faith in the face of persecution — and when persecution comes, they will have the strength to endure it.

North Koreans are suffering from a lack of food. So now

on top of persecution, North Korean believers are facing starvation.

Pray for the leaders of North Korea. Pray for their conversion. If God can do it for Nebuchadnezzar and Saul of Tarsus, God can do it in the hearts of today's leaders.

PHOTO
JOURNAL

Help and Hope for Iraqi refugees

Presenting an Arabic Bible to this Iraqi refugee grandmother and persecuted believer

This Iraqi refugee tries to give me his baby in order to save her life

This persecuted Chinese believer holding his first copy of the Bible

Chinese house church service

Chinese persecuted believer sharing her faith

Persecuted believers praying in a Chinese house church service

These Chinese believers have a passion for the Word of God

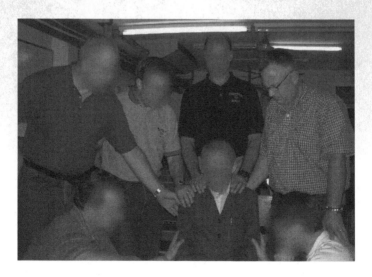

Praying with Pastor Samuel Lamb in China

Chinese persecuted Christian studying the Word

Chinese house church service for persecuted believers

Chinese pastor speaking in a house church

This woman gave me her handwritten copy of the Bible

Persecuted children in Iraq

God's Word is so important to the persecuted church

Chinese persecuted Christians in prayer

The church in Romania where my journey with the persecuted church began

My hero, Samuel Lamb from China

Snowman – a persecuted Chinese pastor and leader of a house church movement

Tom Thompson and Omar, a former fighter with ISIS and now a believer

This Iraqi family of persecuted Christians has suffered greatly for their faith

This Iraqi girl receiving her first copy of the Bible

Iraqi soldiers fighting ISIS

The children are ones who suffer most

Distributing Bibles in Moscow, Russia

An Iraqi refugee camp that houses hundreds of persecuted Christians

Syrian children facing persecution daily

Training Russian pastors, many of whom have been imprisoned for their faith

Worshipping with persecuted Christians in China

North Korea border where 70,000 Christians are in prison camps

South Korean believers praying for their persecuted family members in North Korea

Iraqi believer with a note ISIS nailed to his front door, "Convert, pay, or die"

Many persecuted Christians go hungry every day

5-year-old Mazin cannot speak because of the atrocities he witnessed by ISIS

Presenting this Russian pastor with his first library of Christian books

When you have lost everything, God's Word becomes precious

Providing medical aid to Iraqi persecuted Christians

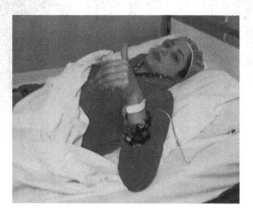

Jordan refugee Amira who suffered burns from an ISIS bomb attack

Tony Foglio training pastors who have suffered tremendous persecution

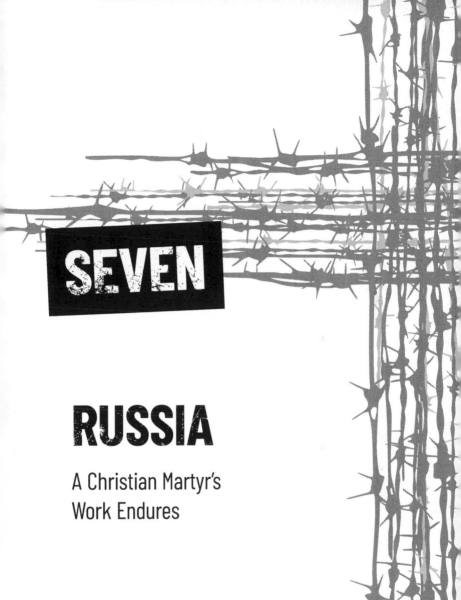

SEVEN

RUSSIA

A Christian Martyr's
Work Endures

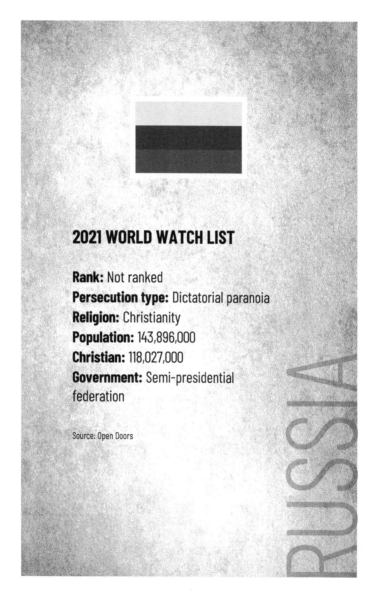

2021 WORLD WATCH LIST

Rank: Not ranked
Persecution type: Dictatorial paranoia
Religion: Christianity
Population: 143,896,000
Christian: 118,027,000
Government: Semi-presidential federation

Source: Open Doors

RUSSIA

That's why I take pleasure in my weaknesses, and in the insults, hardships, persecutions, and troubles that I suffer for Christ. For when I am weak, then I am strong.

— 2 CORINTHIANS 12:10

Although Russia did not make it into Open Door's 2021 list of the top 50 countries where it is most dangerous to be a Christian, the Russian Federation did rank No. 46 in 2020. Christian activity is often under surveillance, and church services are frequently raided. Christian converts — especially those who were followers of Islam — face enormous pressure from family and friends to renounce their faith. Some have even been forced to flee their homes.

And some pay with their lives.

Alexander Menn, 55, was a rather robust man with a thick, salt-and-pepper beard. He was an emerging spiritual leader of the Russian Orthodox Church. Keeping his independence through the Brezhnev years, Menn refused to cooperate with the KGB and endured harassment, interrogations, and threats.

He never faltered in his stand on religious brotherhood and tolerance and spoke on reform, redemption, and self-determination. Alexander was an honest, uncompromising man who offered God's consolation to unbearably hard and empty lives. He loved Jesus Christ, the Russian people, the Russian language, and the Russian culture, and he expressed the Gospel in a way that people loved to hear it. He was well-known and well-loved throughout the U.S.S.R.

Because of that, Alexander was the focus of fear, loathing, and eventually, murder.

Although police cling to the theory that robbery was the motive, evidence points to a different scenario. The blade of an ax was driven into the base of his skull from behind. Murder, not robbery, was the objective. The ax, a horrifying historic symbol of revenge, was also the murder weapon used when Stalin ordered Leon Trotsky eliminated half a century ago.

The stricken Alexander didn't die instantly but staggered toward home and collapsed in a crumpled heap by the fence to his yard. That is where his wife found him — he had bled to death.

To this day, there has been no final investigation into his death. Some believe this is because he died at the hands of the KGB. His crime: the winning of so many new believers who turned their backs on the one creed the state sanctioned — communism.

His killer must now realize what history attests: to create a Christian martyr is to guarantee his work will endure.

Whatever the true facts of his death, Alexander had a burning desire to see his countrymen converted. Even though he is gone, his burden for his people survived and lives on in a special book he wrote right before his death, *To Be a Christian*. In the words of an old Russian proverb, "What is written with a pen cannot be hacked away even by an axe."

To Be a Christian answers, explains, discusses, and defends the Gospel of Jesus Christ in the language, history,

"Early that Sunday morning, Father Alexander Menn closes the front door softly behind him, not to waken his wife, and passes through the gate in the stockade fence. Walking briskly, he crosses the street to a woodland path that leads to the village. The sun is barely above the horizon and the woods are shadowed and cold.

He has followed this routine for a thousand Sundays: the seven-minute walk to the train station to catch the 6:50 local to Moscow; getting off at Pushkino, the market town, to board the No. 24 bus to his parish church in the village of Novaya Derevnya, arriving in good time for the 8 a.m. service.

But not today. Today — September 9, 1990 — his parishioners will wait in vain."[30]

and culture of the Russian people. Because it was written by a fellow Russian, it answers their most important questions: How do you know God exists? Why become a Christian? Why does God allow evil? What is the difference between Christianity and other religions? The book explains the sinless life of Jesus and His death, burial, and resurrection. It also explains the "Christian life," gives a detailed plan of salvation, and ends with an invitation for the reader to personally receive Christ as Savior.

Because Russians deserve to hear the Gospel in their own language and culture, World Help began the monumental task of providing a copy of *To Be a Christian* to every home in Moscow. That calculated to 3 million homes.

The Russian people are highly educated and love to read, but they were raised for two generations under atheism. They have no foundation of belief in God. With the collapse of communism, there exists a spiritual vacuum, and the door is wide open for either the Gospel of Jesus Christ or man-made religions and cults.

Because of the Russians' long history of atheism, they needed more than God's Word; they needed a clear, more exhaustive explanation of the Gospel. They needed the most basic concept: "How to Know God Exists."

To Be a Christian was the "miracle" we needed to help reach the Russian people with the Gospel, and the "Moscow for Jesus" campaign became the vehicle for reaching Moscow.

Our carefully planned mission included a massive

mailing campaign reaching every home in the city of Moscow, a comprehensive pastoral training conference, Bible distribution, humanitarian relief, preaching engagements, and finally, a city-wide crusade in Moscow's Olympic Stadium.

Three million copies of *To Be a Christian* were printed on former communist-owned presses and distributed to the city's 11 million residents, which included 500,000 university students.

Our pastors' conference marked the first occasion in which Russian and American pastors ministered side by side. Nearly 400 Russian pastors and 16 American pastors met for this historic gathering. Attendees arrived from throughout the former Soviet Union, some traveling for several days just to get to the conference.

For more than 70 years, it was illegal for Russian pastors to meet. But now that there was a degree of religious freedom, most could not afford the expense of a trip to Moscow. World Help paid for the Russian pastors' travel expenses, meals, and lodging, making it possible for them to attend.

Each pastor received a 186-page notebook with the outlines of each session translated into Russian. After each session and during every break, the Russian pastors crowded around the Americans and engaged in spirited question-and-answer sessions — they were hungry to learn. The pastors had no libraries to speak of, so World Help presented each pastor with more than 200 Christian books, Bibles, and commentaries.

With tears in his eyes, one Russian pastor said, "I have been praying for a concordance for over two years, and now I finally have one."

They also received copies of the Russian version of the *JESUS* film. More than 6 billion people have seen the film in over 200 countries, and more than 200 million people have indicated decisions to follow Christ after watching the film.[31]

According to the U.S. Center for World Missions, "No single evangelistic campaign in human history has touched as many lives as the showing of this film worldwide."[32]

We also conducted a city-wide evangelistic program. Five teams of American pastors and church leaders penetrated the 100 square miles of Moscow and distributed more than 200,000 Bibles and Christian books in evangelistic services. They gave more than $60,000 worth of basic medical supplies to hospitals that were hard-pressed to find even aspirin or rubber gloves.

The teams encountered communities that had never heard an American speaker, churches that had never hosted

"I have been praying for a concordance for over two years, and now I finally have one."

any foreign visitor, and orphanages and schools that had never heard the Gospel.

Finally, more than 10,000 people attended the campaign's closing rally at Olympic Stadium. The rally featured a musical drama with a huge cast of actors and an original score. A 10-minute video depicted one of Alexander Menn's last sermons, including biblical scenes and illustrations.

Everyone who attended the gathering received a Russian New Testament and a copy of Alexander's 320-page book, *The Son of Man*, a chronicle of the life of Christ.

Nearly 5,000 people stood at the close of the service and became followers of Jesus Christ. We had a total of 7,756 recorded decisions in 10 days.

It was a new day in Russia. The doors of freedom had swung wide open and the Word of God came flooding in.

HOW YOU CAN PRAY

Pray for guidance for Russia's Christians that they will comply with their country's laws while ministering to others and sharing the Gospel message.

The average Russian was raised with the belief that spiritual matters should remain private; most believe they are saved by their good works. Pray that the Holy Spirit will work in the hearts of these people and make them receptive to His Word.

Pray for the safety of church members when they are arrested and questioned by police.

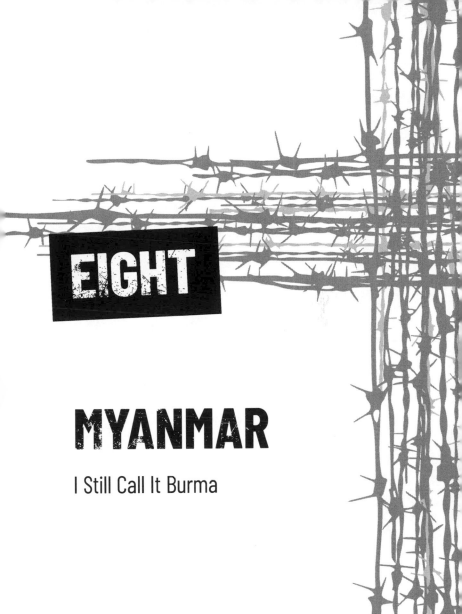

EIGHT

MYANMAR

I Still Call It Burma

2021 WORLD WATCH LIST

Rank: #18
Persecution type: Religious nationalism
Religion: Buddhism
Persecution level: Very high
Population: 54,808,000
Christian: 4,362,000
Government: Parliamentary Republic

Source: Open Doors

MYANMAR

For you have been given not only the privilege of trusting in Christ but also the privilege of suffering for him.

— PHILIPPIANS 1:29

David Yone Mo was once the leader of a violent, notorious street gang, a drug addict — a man with just days left to live.

He contracted viral hepatitis from using dirty heroin needles. The disease ravaged his body to the point that his doctor sent David's mother home to begin making funeral preparations.

His diagnosis — David would be dead within a week.

Before leaving, David's mother — a devout Christian — left a Bible under his pillow. Realizing that his death was imminent, he began reading.

As he read the words of Jesus to the dying thief on the cross, *"Today you will be with me in paradise,"* God broke through his hardened heart and David gave his life to Christ. He immediately felt God's healing power surge through his body. He knew God had saved him and healed him.

After his miraculous transformation, David led his friends and former gang members to Christ. Many of his former drug buddies entered God's kingdom, one by one. Soon they formed a new "gang" — the Myanmar Young

Crusaders. Little did they know in what a mighty way God was going to use them.

> More than **100,000** Christians in the northern part of Myanmar live in internal displacement camps (IDPs) where they are deprived of access to food and health care.
>
> Source: Open Doors

After the military crackdown in 1989, the government changed the name of their country to Myanmar, but I still call it Burma. Many countries throughout the world have never officially recognized the name change.

In this nation of over 54 million people, approximately 8 percent of the population professes Christ.

The people of Burma are intensely religious. In a land filled with beautiful gold-covered temples, the people are oppressed by the darkness of false religion and the enslavement of drug abuse. It is estimated that two out of every three young people in Burma are drug addicts.

During my first visit, I had the opportunity to minister in the Mayangyaung leper colony located about 50 miles from Yangon, the capital city. We were only the second group of foreigners allowed to visit.

Approximately 100 Christian families are among the

residents of this colony situated at the end of a nearly deserted road. It was established by the government in an attempt to isolate — some say forget — the more than 3,000 residents stricken with this dreaded disease.

I was totally overwhelmed by these mostly forgotten brothers and sisters in Christ who suffer terribly with this disease but love Christ with all their hearts.

We also were privileged to dedicate a church that was planted the previous year. It already had 125 members.

Perhaps the most important part of my trip was conducting an intensive leadership training conference for 150 Burmese pastors.

The conference was crucial in reaching Burma with the Gospel, because the government has declared that no foreign missionaries are allowed in their country. I realized that the work of evangelism and discipleship must be done by national pastors — or it will not be done at all.

Many of these pastors traveled for hours just to receive training in God's Word. They have a great desire to reach their people with the Gospel.

These courageous men face extreme persecution and danger every day. God is using them to break down the strongholds of Buddhism, Hinduism, and Islam, but not without danger to themselves and their families' lives.

Many pastors are persecuted by the government. Others are disowned by their families or beaten and driven out of towns and villages where they try to establish a church.

Most of these pastors, if not all, have given up everything for the sake of the Gospel. They labor tirelessly despite persecution and hardship, but I have never heard even one of them complain.

I met one young pastor, a former drug addict, who found he was infected with AIDS. He has endured numerous beatings, death threats, and endless persecution for planting three churches in Amar — a city without a Christian witness of any kind.

As we prayed together, the pastor's words brought tears to my eyes. He said, "God, my life is in Your hands. I know my days are numbered, but in the time I have left, I want to serve You."

I also met a 28-year-old man who studied Buddhist scripture for four years and served as a Buddhist monk for eight years.

Despite devotion to his religion, he felt empty. He tried his best to obey the laws of his false religion but fell short. He found no comfort in reincarnation and often wondered if there were more to life after death than an endless, repeating cycle.

He kept asking himself, "What will fill the void I have in my heart?"

He finally attended a Christian church in his monk's robes, looking for spiritual answers. He received a Burmese Bible, and as he read these verses, he found the answers he sought. *"Come to me, all you who are weary and burdened, and I will give you rest"*[33] and *"Whoever lives and believes in me will never die."*[34]

This young man became a Christian, attended four years of Bible college, and is serving Christ today as a pastor in Burma.

I met him again a year later at our pastors' conference outside the city of Mandalay. He told me, "I have a heart for evangelism. I want to reach the Buddhists in Burma. I know how to witness to them because I was once a Buddhist priest."

The Myanmar Young Crusaders — the group David Yone Mo founded — sponsor numerous evangelistic crusades each year. They have started 200 churches in the past 20 years. They also direct three Bible colleges, operate an orphanage where they care for more than 100 children, minister in a large leper colony, provide HIV/AIDS hospice care, and direct a drug rehabilitation program with a success rate of 80 percent.

The key to success in their drug program is the requirement that participants read the Bible, attend daily prayer meetings, and attend Bible college classes. Many graduates of the program are now missionaries in Burma.

> "God, my life is in Your hands. I know my days are numbered, but in the time I have left, I want to serve You."

I've been to Burma many times, but I will always remember my visit to the church founded by one of the greatest missionaries of all time, Adoniram Judson, who lived and died more than 100 years ago.

Judson and his wife labored for more than two years in Burma before finding an opportunity to share Christ. After six long years, only one person came to Christ. Judson labored in Burma for nearly 40 years, and when he died in 1850, there were only 10 Burmese believers. Looking objectively at his ministry, many would consider Adoniram Judson[35] a dismal failure. History has proven otherwise.

One of the greatest accomplishments of Judson's life was the translation of Scripture into the Burmese language. His painstaking work was so accurate it remains the translation of choice among Burmese Christians.

Judson traveled to Burma in 1812 as America's first foreign missionary. He persevered in his mission despite personal tragedy, government persecution, and discouraging results. He is hailed today as the "spiritual father" to Burmese believers.

David knew I collected Bibles from around the world, and as a parting gift after one of my trips, he gave me a Burmese Bible. I quickly thumbed through it but couldn't read a word. It was all in Burmese, except for the title page, which was in English. It read, "Translated by A. Judson."

He asked if I knew who Adoniram Judson was. I quickly said, "Of course!"

David looked at me and said something I'll never forget.

"When Adoniram Judson came to my country there were no Christians — none! Today, there are more than 6 million Christians in Burma, and every one of them, without exception, can trace their spiritual heritage back to one man, an American by the name of Adoniram Judson."

David was diagnosed with liver cancer in April 2002 and underwent treatment in Singapore. The doctors gave him a 50-50 chance of survival, yet he never lost hope.

After many months of courageous struggle, David lost his battle with cancer on Aug. 24, 2003. God called one of my heroes home.

HOW YOU CAN PRAY

Pray for Christians in Myanmar that God would give them wisdom and discernment as they deal with challenging circumstances on many levels.

Pray that believers would be bold in sharing their faith despite the consequences.

Pray that simple forms of Christian worship will sprout into multiplying movements across the nation.

NINE

IRAQ

Founded on Persecution

2021 WORLD WATCH LIST

Rank: #11
Persecution type: Islamic oppression
Religion: Islam
Persecution level: Extreme
Population: 41,503,000
Christian: 175,000
Government: Federal Parliamentary Republic

Source: Open Doors

IRAQ

I am glad when I suffer for you in my body, for I am participating in the sufferings of Christ that continue for his body, the church   — COLOSSIANS 1:24

For almost 2,000 years Christians and Muslims peacefully coexisted, despite times of intermittent, sometimes harsh, persecution. Christians in Syria and Iraq are considered among the oldest, continuous Christian communities in the world.

The relationship between Christians and Muslims in the Middle East varies greatly from country to country and even within countries. Even where there are good, relatively peaceful relationships, there is an undercurrent of tensions that permeates these relationships — especially for Christians.

Christianity in the Middle East was founded on persecution. When persecution against the church in Jerusalem broke out in the first century, believers fled across the region. Acts 8:4 says *"But the believers who were scattered preached the Good News about Jesus wherever they went."*

Tradition has it that the Apostle Thomas is the one who brought Christianity to Iraq. The Assyrian Christian community prides itself on speaking and worshipping in Aramaic, the common Middle Eastern language spoken during Jesus' lifetime.

But beginning in 2003, following the Second Gulf War, Christian/Muslim relationships in Iraq began to rapidly deteriorate as open attacks against Christians by extremist groups became more frequent — and deadly. Bombings of churches became common. Christians were afraid to venture out in public, even to go to the market, for fear that they would be targeted.

As attacks and threats increased, over half the Christians living in southern Iraq fled, heading either to other countries or to the Kurdish region of northern Iraq. Prior to the war there were approximately 1.2 million Christians in Iraq. Today, there are an estimated 175,000 Christians remaining, most now living in the Kurdish region.

Scattered across the Nineveh Plain in northern Iraq are numerous predominantly Christian communities where Christians and Muslims had been living side by side for centuries. This includes Mosul, Iraq's second largest city after Baghdad. Those fleeing the violence of southern Iraq felt that they could find shelter and peace within these Christian communities.

But then ISIS arrived on the scene ...

THE CHRISTIAN HOLOCAUST

"Convert, pay, or die."

These chilling words were blasted on loudspeakers stationed on every corner of the northern Iraqi city of Mosul ... where thousands of Christians had fled for their lives.

It was October 2014 and ISIS (Islamic State of Iraq and Syria) had seized control of Mosul.

Thousands of innocent civilians had been murdered in cold blood.

The extremist group specifically targeted Christians for mass executions, giving each the choice to "convert or die." Many people, including children, gave their lives in the name of Christ.

Churches dating back to the first and second centuries, along with other ancient holy sites, like the tomb of Jonah, were systematically targeted and destroyed.

The Arabic symbol "nun" is the 14th letter of their alphabet and serves as the equivalent of our letter "N." The symbol was used by ISIS to mark property belonging to Christians or "Nazarenes," which was to be confiscated or destroyed.

Men and boys were rounded up, blindfolded, and executed at mass burial sites.

Women and girls were abducted, sold into marriage, or kept in captivity to be used for heinous acts of sexual violence. Some children were kidnapped and forced to become child soldiers, suicide bombers, and human shields in a vicious war in which there were no real winners.

Many called it "the Christian Holocaust."[36]

A pastor shared with me the heartbreaking story of families who had lost their children during ISIS's attack on the Christian town of Qaraqosh:

"The village was bombed, and the Christians were forced to flee or face imminent death.

"They (ISIS soldiers) went to one family where the kids were told to convert or be killed. They refused. There were four of them, 15 years and younger. They beheaded all of them. They were all our children. That is how evil these people are. They have no respect for anyone. The other day, they cut a 4-year-old boy in half. He didn't do anything. What kind of threat was he? He was just a child ..."

Water and electricity were cut off. Church steeples with crosses were knocked down and all Christian symbols were removed throughout the church and compound. The interior courtyard of the largest church in Qaraqosh was used for target practice by ISIS.

ISIS purposely used churches as their headquarters to show that they were now the religious authorities. Reports of mass beheadings of entire families of Christ-followers — even children — were confirmed by numerous news agencies stationed inside the region.

Today, thousands of people, mostly believers who managed to escape, continue to live in refugee camps.

I also heard about Bhandawa, a village of Christians on the Ninevah Plain that had been cut off. They were starving — they hadn't had food or supplies in weeks. We quickly organized a caravan filled with food, water, medicine, blankets, and other supplies and headed their way.

After several hours of driving and several military check points, I began to get nervous. I asked the head of our security why it was taking so long. He showed me the iPad he was using for GPS navigation, and I was shocked to discover that Bhandawa was a village just outside of Mosul.

Then I remembered Mosul was the Old Testament city of Ninevah, and much of the Nineveh Plain was under the administrative control of Mosul.

We were headed straight for ISIS!

> "They (ISIS soldiers) went to one family where the kids were told to convert or be killed. They refused. There were four of them, 15 years and younger. They beheaded all of them."

When we arrived in Bhandawa, I was told that we only had a little over an hour to distribute the aid. Many of the Christians in this village had fled here after they were driven out of their homes in Mosul by ISIS. The majority of them were robbed of any of their belongings at checkpoints along the way. With nothing left to call their own, the kindness of strangers was their only hope for survival.

These refugees were bewildered, starving, sick, and utterly alone. Every day they lived in fear. Their children cried out in the night, terrified by nightmares of the horrors they witnessed — astonishing images of evil that can never be erased.

I quickly discovered that the night before we arrived, ISIS had fired artillery in the field adjacent to the village. Suddenly, less than 200 yards from us, two artillery shells exploded. In the middle of our aid distribution, the head of our security said urgently, "We must go. We must go now!"

I quickly gathered hundreds of Iraqi Christians together, prayed for them, and we left.

I had nearly come face to face with the evil of ISIS.

Seeing the desperation and hopelessness of the people in Iraq firsthand was indescribable.

Every single Christian I met had a story of suffering and intense persecution.

The refugees recounted story after story of how they made their way from war-torn Syria and Iraq.

Almost everyone had someone in their family who was killed or captured. Walking away from their homes, their jobs — everything they had ever known — they gathered remaining loved ones and made the long journey across the desert — taking an average of 30-45 days — to be smuggled across the border.

Some couldn't hold back the tears, while others stared blankly ahead, too traumatized to express any emotion other than utter shock.

DESPERATION OF A FATHER

In one refugee camp, I saw a man hurrying toward me carrying a tiny baby in his arms. He kept pleading with me to do something, but I couldn't understand him. When he finally reached me, he began to push the baby into my arms, repeating the same words over and over.

I quickly learned that his wife had been killed, and he had been trying to keep his 3-month-old daughter alive by himself in the bitter cold temperatures. He said it had been raining and snowing for weeks and food was running out.

He was afraid the baby was dying — he wanted me to take her so her life might be spared.

He was trying to give me his own daughter.

I stood there, stunned. Dear God … This man has just lost his wife, and he's about to lose his baby, too. He would rather give her to me — a total stranger — than risk having her die in his arms.

I took the man to one of our partners on the ground and promised him we would do all we could to help him and his daughter. And then, with tears in my eyes, I had to walk away as I tried to regain my composure. It was a moment I will never forget.

I thought about my own children. I can't even fathom handing one of them over to a stranger as an adult, let alone, as a child. I was in the midst of a most desperate situation. I was staring into the face of hopelessness.

FORCED TO DO THE UNTHINKABLE

Torture. Murder. Rape. It's hard to believe that people could be capable of such evil. And it's no wonder that nearly 3 million Iraqis fled their homes to escape this violence — and many are still living in refugee camps today.

I'll warn you, the story I'm about to share is gruesome. But we can't hide or turn away from the horrors of this unyielding evil.

After ISIS captured a young woman, they took her baby from her and starved the young mother for three days. When they finally offered her a plate of food, she eagerly ate it, not knowing when her next meal would arrive.

It was only then that her cruel guards looked down at her and said, "We cooked your 1-year-old son, and this is what you just ate."

She was horrified.

Stories like this are all too common in Iraq and Syria. These people have endured more than we can ever imagine.

SCARED SPEECHLESS

I met a 5-year-old boy named Mazin.

I learned Mazin's story from his uncle, who had to speak for him. Before long, I understood the sobering truth: This little boy was too traumatized to even speak. In fact, he hadn't spoken a word in weeks.

> "He's seen too many horrors to overcome them. Please pray for him ... for us."

Mazin's uncle explained that his nephew, one of six children, once enjoyed a full and happy childhood before ISIS soldiers took over his village of Qaraquosh in northern Iraq.

"He was creative, active, adventurous, talkative, and fun-loving [before ISIS came]," the uncle explains. "We lived a normal life in a nice home with many members of our extended family." As he speaks, Mazin's mother sobs uncontrollably by her son's side.

ISIS immediately began executing Christians in the streets for refusing to convert to radical Islam. Mazin saw horrific acts of violence — beheadings, torture, murder — and has never been the same since, so traumatized that he became mute and unresponsive even to his mother.

The family fled from their home and sought refuge in an abandoned bakery in a Kurdish community in Iraq before finally crossing the border into Jordan.

As foreigners, they have no way to earn a living, forcing Mazin's father to remain in Iraq to send back the little he is able to earn.

I watched as Mazin stared blankly ahead, too broken inside to speak. Even though he never said a word, this child's voice was more powerful than any other I heard that day.

"He's seen too many horrors to overcome them," Mazin's uncle said, grief-stricken. "Please pray for him . . . for us." I promised him that I would.

I walked away with a broken heart. This little boy, with his whole future ahead of him, lives every day haunted by horrifying images that no human being should ever have to be exposed to or experience. I have a grandson his age. I immediately thought of him and how devastated I would be if this were happening to him.

"YOU WILL CONVERT TO ISLAM!"

Nadal and her husband knew it was only a matter of time before ISIS descended upon their village just outside of Qaraqosh, Iraq.

As Christians, they knew they couldn't stay in the area. They had heard of the atrocities ISIS had committed against other Christ-followers. Nadal shuddered when she thought of what had happened to children the same age as her own three daughters.

No evil was beyond ISIS — they were capable of virtually anything. But Nadal trusted God.

Then one day without warning, ISIS members arrived in the village. They went from door to door checking for weapons but assured Nadal they would not disturb her family. "You are Christian people. We will not hurt you," they promised. Still, they would not allow the family to leave the village until they received orders from their superiors, and Nadal knew the ISIS occupation could only stay peaceful for so long.

They had to flee before it was too late.

About a month after ISIS arrived, Nadal and her family discreetly traveled to a local checkpoint leading to the major route they must take toward safety — praying with all their might they would be allowed to pass. Miraculously, they were approved, but trouble was far from over. There was one more checkpoint several miles away that they would still need to pass through.

Shortly after arriving at the second checkpoint, they were arrested along with another family, and their IDs and cell phones were confiscated. Just when they thought they were about to make their final escape, their hopes were dashed.

"You will be Muslim people. You will convert to Islam!"

an officer barked at her family.

"No. We will stay Christian," Nadal declared resolutely.

Tensions were high as the parties deliberated. In a heated moment, one of the militants grabbed Nadal's 7-year-old daughter and brutally shoved her into a wall causing her to scream in pain and terror.

"You will be Muslim people. You will convert to Islam!"

After negotiating with the officers, they were given an ultimatum. If Nadal and her daughters wanted to live, her husband would have to stay behind as an ISIS prisoner. Their daughters began to wail with fear upon hearing their father was not leaving with them.

Nadal could only sob in horror. Yet she knew ISIS was capable of much worse — if they stayed, she and her daughters might be killed or sold as brides to militants.

She had no choice but to trust her husband's life to God's care and continue their journey to safety without him.

Today, Nadal and her family live in a refugee community in Iraq. She hasn't seen her husband in years but has heard rumors of his death.

"The children cry every night, begging for their father to return," she said.

Despite everything her family has endured, Nadal told

us she still has hope. She has not lost her faith in God. And like so many Iraqi Christians, their faith alone sustains them.

FORCED TO FLEE

George and Amal are good examples of a persecuted brother and sister you can pray for today. A member of our team met George not long ago, and his story is shocking. They have been through worse persecution than you or I can even imagine.

This is George and Amal's story of faith, fright, and flight.

One of George's regular customers for his taxi was a very strict Muslim family who always called when they needed a ride somewhere. Because George was a Christian, they trusted him and allowed him to take their daughter, Amal, to a certain place on a weekly basis and ensure that she got there safely.

One day, George picked her up and safely got her to her destination. However, after she got out of the car and walked away, he noticed in the rear-view mirror that Amal got into another taxi. He was worried about this and decided to follow that taxi without her noticing because he felt that if something happened to her the parents would blame him.

George was surprised when the taxi stopped at a church where she got out and went in. He left his car and followed Amal inside where he found her praying and crying out to God. He was shocked, especially since she normally wore a hijab like any faithful Muslim woman would wear. However, now she had her hijab off.

When he approached her, she was terrified and started crying.

He told her, "Do not worry, it will be fine. I will not inform your family. However, I am curious to know how you ended up coming to the church and accepting Jesus as your Savior?"

She replied, "By the radio. I started texting them and they led me to this church. Please help me. I want to be baptized."

Because Amal was from a strict Muslim family, the church was afraid to baptize her at that time. George gave her his Bible and drove her back home.

A week later, however, her parents found out about her secret. They found the Bible with George's name on it in her bag. They called George, pretending they needed his taxi services, asking him to meet them at a deserted location.

All the male members of the extended family were there, and they grabbed George and stabbed him multiple times in his shoulders and back, leaving him for dead on the side of the road. Someone found him and took him to the hospital where, without any painkillers, he received 22 stitches for his wounds.

After this, George and Amal became faithful friends. And although they could not date for fear of what her parents would do, they were able to see one another secretly.

However, when the parents learned of this, they had George arrested. While a lawyer was able to get release papers signed, the family paid off the police who kept him in jail for over a year, telling him he would be there until he died.

But God wonderfully intervened when he was "accidentally" transferred to another police station — and they honored the release papers.

Shortly after his release, the two friends were able to find a pastor who was willing to baptize Amal. He first met with her to discuss what baptism meant and to get to know her better.

Afterward he told George, "You need to marry her. God will prosper you." George really didn't have a plan for that at the time, but he did think it would be a good idea. They were married on the spot.

Amal's family immediately began to persecute them. Various family members followed them everywhere, finally showing up at their home one day when George wasn't there to kidnap Amal and their newborn child. They beat Amal and dragged her across the floor, opening up the stitches from her recent caesarean birth.

When George found out where they had taken his wife and child, he immediately went to rescue his family. While he was getting them into his car, Amal's family tried to pull her back out, breaking her arm in the process.

They began beating George, but neighbors intervened not knowing what was happening, allowing George to escape with his family.

The couple knew they could no longer remain where they were and fled first to Lebanon, and for the past few years have been living in Germany.

However, they are having difficulty getting their residency papers as the woman who first interviewed them was a Muslim who was shocked that Amal had become a Christian and didn't believe it could happen. While they are both exhausted from the stress, they are still serving the Lord with strong faith.

MINISTRY CAME AT A STEEP COST

I met Yusuf in 2006 shortly after a trip to the Middle East. Being burdened for Iraq, I was seeking someone with whom we could partner. In a providential meeting at a missions conference we were both speaking at in Minnesota, we became instant friends.

Yusuf pastored what was to become the largest church in Baghdad — by 2010 the attendance exceeded 1,000. Through his ministry we were able to provide hundreds of thousands of Bibles and New Testaments for Iraqis, help fund church construction, and assist with leadership training.

The success of Yusuf's ministry came at a steep cost. Muslim extremists took notice of what was being accomplished and threatened his life if he did not stop what he was doing. The threats and living in constant fear took a toll on Yusuf, and he suffered a heart attack.

The daily tensions also impacted his wife, Nylah, and their three children. Their oldest son was getting personal threats at school because he had been sharing his faith. The threats became so concerning that Yusuf and Nylah decided to send him to neighboring Jordan to stay with friends and attend school there.

One morning before taking his youngest son to school, Yusuf noticed that his backpack looked fuller than usual. When he asked his son about it, the boy replied that he was beginning to carry his pajamas, toothbrush, and other daily essentials with him. He explained that in case both his father and mother were killed, he had the things with him he needed to be able to stay with someone else.

With the increasing nature of the threats, Yusuf and Nylah's concern for the care and safety of their children brought about a hard decision. At no time, outside of their own home, would they do anything together as a family unit. Nylah began homeschooling.

And Yusuf and Nylah never went anywhere together. Yusuf would drive nervously to church, constantly scanning the street for any indication of danger. Nylah would leave the house only to go to the market, quickly picking up what she needed, and going straight back home. The thought was that if anything happened and one of them was killed, the other would still be there for the children.

The stress and strain of living under constant threats to their lives became unbearable. How do you go about normal life knowing there are people who want to kill you? Yusuf was receiving almost daily threats on his phone or with notes left at his doorstep or at the church. Nylah got to the point where she no longer left the house for any reason.

One evening around 8 p.m. I was moved to give Yusuf a phone call to see how he was doing. I didn't even think about the fact that there was a six-hour time difference – I was calling him at 2 a.m. his time! But he and the entire family were wide awake.

Earlier in the evening Yusuf was in their enclosed courtyard playing with his son and daughter when the son suddenly noticed a red dot moving across his father's chest – the targeting laser dot of a sniper's rifle! He warned his father in time and they fled inside the house.

But the night got even worse. Hearing a commotion in the street outside their home, Yusuf decided to call the police. However, before the police could arrive, terrorists struck; but they went to the wrong house. His neighbor had the same name as Yusuf. The terrorists dragged him into the street, killed him, and then placed his body in a box and lit it on fire.

The police were still with Yusuf when I called. The local police chief was a friend of Yusuf's and said he would post a 24-hour guard on the house. But, would that be enough to protect him and his family?

As I talked with Yusuf, he broke down crying. The stress was overwhelming. After praying with him and offering empty sounding words of encouragement, I got off the phone with him and immediately called one of our team members who worked with our Middle East partners. I told him about the situation and said do whatever you have to, but we need to get Yusuf and his family out of Iraq!

My phone call with Yusuf was early on a Tuesday morning. By Friday night, our team member was on a plane headed to Turkey where we had arranged for the family to flee. They left Iraq with just 13 suitcases, leaving behind all the rest of their belongings.

And for Yusuf, the hardest thing he left behind was his ministry. We were able to help get them settled in Turkey, finding housing, purchasing furniture, and most importantly, showing them love and care.

There is, however, a positive side for Yusuf and for other believers who have been forced to flee the violence of the Middle East. Just like the Christians in the early church fleeing persecution in Jerusalem, Christians fleeing persecution in places like Iraq are sharing the Gospel with other refugees in the locations to which they fled.

While in Turkey, Yusuf started an Arab-language church and a leadership training program for refugees from both Iraq and Syria.

After living as a refugee in Turkey for three years, Yusuf and his family were able to emigrate to Australia where he soon began another Arab-language church for the many refugees who were living there, along with continuing the leadership training program both locally and through social media.

Individuals whom Yusuf trained are now serving as pastors and leaders in churches around the world. While being forced to flee their home and country, they still rejoice in God's goodness and care. What terrorists meant for evil, God has used for good.

ANNIHILATING CHRISTIANITY

I met Karam and Rana, a couple who lived in Mosul before it was overrun by ISIS.

A notice had been pinned on their door, confirming the worst: **Any Christians left in Mosul would be executed in the streets for apostasy.**

Karam and Rana gathered their children and ran, moving constantly to escape the slaughter. In all, they've lived in four different villages without hope for safety or consistency anywhere. They told me, "Our children have no way to go to school; we have nowhere to live; we have no solutions; there is nothing to go back to.

"This is the end for Christians in Iraq," Karam said. "All of us are leaving."

My emotions were on overload as I thought about his words. No more Christians in Iraq? We couldn't sit by and let that happen. We had to do something!

THEY RAN FOR THEIR LIVES

Saleem and his family are from the village of Shangal in northern Iraq. When ISIS marched through Saleem's hometown, homes and businesses were ransacked and all weapons confiscated.

Civilians were mercilessly harassed and attacked for owning anything "illegal," and were stripped of any valuables they had.

"Our children have no way to go to school; we have nowhere to live; we have no solutions; there is nothing to go back to."

Then the murders began. Children ran, screaming with terror. Mangled bodies lay scattered in the streets where packs of hungry dogs tore them apart.

Saleem frantically gathered his wife and 10 children, cramming them into one vehicle to escape. His 14-year-old son has special needs, making it very difficult for him to walk, so Saleem carried him. They brought no belongings, no money, no food, no water.

All they had left were their lives — and they, too, were hanging in the balance.

Finally, they reached the tent cities of Ainkawa — located just outside of Erbil, the capital of Kurdistan — where they live in utter desolation. Saleem was unable to find work and relies solely on the generosity of strangers to feed his children. They were forced to rummage through garbage just to survive.

"I'm grateful we are safe from ISIS. Only months ago, I had a successful job, a home, and money to feed my family. Now, I am a scavenger with no options left," he told me, hanging his head in shame and sorrow.

I tried to put myself in Saleem's shoes — picturing what it must feel like to have no way to provide for your wife and children. My heart broke for him — the desperation he must feel. I didn't think I could handle any more stories like this, but they just kept coming.

"OUR LIVES ARE EMPTY HERE"

Shahad, a mother of five from Mosul, is struggling to keep her young family alive.

When ISIS infiltrated the city, she and her husband watched in horror as friends and neighbors were forced to convert to radical Islam under penalty of death.

Many refused and were brutally executed. She and her family fled to another village miles away. Not long after, ISIS took over this village, as well, and Shahad's husband was shot.

In the same chaotic moment, some of the soldiers grabbed the couple's 6-year-old daughter and threatened to kidnap her or make the family watch the soldiers take turns raping her.

Shahad pleaded and prayed to God, and miraculously the soldiers left.

Wounded and unable to run, her husband begged Shahad to flee Iraq with the children — their only hope of safety. They are now struggling to survive alone with nowhere to turn.

"I tell my children to look to Jesus for protection, but our lives are empty here," she told me as she wept.

HE CAN'T PROVIDE FOR HIS FAMILY

Raad, his wife Entisar, and their four children were one of the families we were able to help.

Originally from Qaraqosh, the family fled when ISIS infiltrated their city and began killing civilians. As bombs began to drop, they piled into their car and drove north.

They were forced to abandon their car at a Kurdish roadblock and were forced to proceed on foot. Raad had to carry his disabled daughter (who cannot walk) for miles

> "We are thankful to be alive and actually feel much safer in this area. But our children still cry at night from flashbacks of ISIS' attack on our village. Our neighbors help strengthen our faith. We are holding fast to the verse that says, 'You will be persecuted because of me...'"

while his wife held their newborn son.

When I met them, they had lived in an abandoned church, in tents, and everywhere in between. Every location presented a new challenge to care for their special-needs daughter, who hadn't had access to the care she so desperately needed.

Two villages and two displacements later, they now lived in a tiny room with several other families.

With so many displaced, there is no work available for Raad, and he worries about providing for his daughter, who requires extensive care. My heart broke when I heard him speak these words:

"We are thankful to be alive and actually feel much safer in this area. But our children still cry at night from flashbacks of ISIS' attack on our village. Our neighbors help strengthen our faith. We are holding fast to the verse that says, 'You will be persecuted because of me ...'"

The sincerity of his faith challenged me to the core. I asked him if there was a message he had for the church in

America. This was his powerful response:

> "Pray God would protect us. Pray God would bring us back home. Pray God would show us a way out of this darkness."

I cannot relate to being brutally persecuted for my faith. I won't even pretend to know the kind of suffering these families endure. But as the body of Christ, we are all part of the same family.

If one part hurts, we all hurt. This is a sign of solidarity ... of unity ... of hope in a God who is strong enough to comfort and protect His people.

It reminds me to pray. It reminds me to trust. It reminds me that I cannot afford to be complacent in my faith when my brothers and sisters are dying for theirs.

BETRAYAL AFTER ISIS

They thought they were safe when ISIS was driven out of their village. But for Robar and Swalene — Christians living in a predominantly Muslim town near Mosul — the real persecution had only begun.

Robar was a truck driver who also owned his home and farm. He and his wife grew small crops of vegetables and raised livestock. Things weren't always easy, but life was good and full of possibilities for their children.

But ISIS changed all that.

Trucks filled with militants poured into town, but Iraqi forces soon mounted a counterattack ... and eventually drove ISIS away. Those were dark days for Robar's family — they hid in their home, terrified as a battle literally raged around them.

Although ISIS was gone, their hostility remained. Robar and Swalene's Muslim neighbors suddenly became ruthless — they embraced ISIS ideology and demanded that Christians either convert to Islam or pay a hefty tax.

After refusing their ultimatums multiple times, Robar grew uneasy for his family. Panic and hostility were spreading, and deep down, he knew violence was imminent.

"It was always difficult to be surrounded by people of an extremely different faith, but now it's impossible, after they took everything from us," Robar said.

So, Robar and Swalene packed up their children and what little they could carry and fled in the night.

Now, everything is difficult for them — Robar has

Many Christians forced to flee during the height of ISIS' power are still refugees, and those who remain face tremendous discrimination and persecution from radical Muslims, the government, and even family and friends. In the early 2000s there were close to 1.5 million Iraqi Christians. Today, because of displacement by ISIS, only **175,000** remain.

Source: Open Doors

no job and no home for his family. They take comfort in the encouragement and prayers of Christians around the world. But the hardest part is the sting of betrayal and the knowledge that they can never return home … life as they knew it is gone.

LAST TO LEAVE

The streets were eerily quiet as Monther and his family stood outside their home for the last time.

Out of habit, Monther locked the door, even though he knew it would do little to stop looters or extremists. Looking around the neighborhood he knew so well, Monther strained his ears for the whistle of explosives or the crackle of gunfire — any sign of life. The once bustling city of Hamdania was abandoned, and Monther's family was the last to leave.

For once, the world was silent and empty as a tomb.

Prior to ISIS, Monther was a driver for the government and a security guard at a local Christian church. Even as ISIS militants and Kurdish soldiers fought for control of the city, Monther's family stubbornly stayed put out of love for their church family and their home.

But staying came at a cost: Monther's family witnessed a bomb hit a nearby home — and found the mangled, lifeless bodies of their neighbors amid the rubble.

Torn between his desire to protect his church and fear for what ISIS would do to his children if they were found, Monther eventually decided it was time to flee.

His entire family relocated to two rooms above an abandoned building where they sell items to other refugees.

While they're grateful for the warmth their home provides, food is scarce, and the children aren't in school.

Monther's family prays that someday soon they can return home to their beloved church and live in safety. But before that can happen, much of their city will have to be rebuilt. "We must stand on our own two feet again. We just need help to get back up."

ABANDONED DREAMS

At least we are warm," Adnan reminds himself when the enormity of his family's suffering weighs heavily on him. As a father, he feels a constant undercurrent of frustration as he watches his children. "I am supposed to protect them," he often thinks. "But how can I?"

Back when his wife, Nawal, and their six children lived in Mosul, he was an engineer for the government. Today, his university degree is useless because an internally displaced person is restricted from work because of a shortage of jobs.

Adnan's oldest son has a full scholarship to medical school, but he has decided not to pursue his education. Instead, he's trying to find work to help support the family. One of Adnan's other children has special needs, but the family can't afford the specialized care he requires.

After fleeing Mosul, the family spent weeks living in a churchyard before being moved to a refugee settlement where the conditions were horrendous, and the cold was unbearable.

They lived on the top floor of an abandoned mall that was owned by a Christian businessman until it closed in

2018. They are completely reliant on the support of others for basic needs like food and water.

Despite these hardships, the family's faith in God remains their source of strength. Adnan and Nawal hang crosses everywhere — on their door, in the hallways, and in their room as a sign of their trust in God.

Right now, their prayer is simple: That they will live to see their city revived again. They dream of a day when Mosul will once again be full of life and light.

THERE IS HOPE

My friend Tom Thompson and I have traveled to Turkey numerous times to help train and encourage persecuted believers. It was on one of those trips that Tom met Omar in the city of Yalova.

Omar was once a persecutor of Christians, but now he is an example of God's grace and forgiveness.

"Omar fled to Turkey after being a fighter with ISIS while in Mosul, Iraq," Tom recalls. "Though he was in line to be the head of ISIS in Mosul, he had become disillusioned with all ISIS stood for and fled to Turkey.

"He happened to meet our Iraqi partners while walking the street of Yalova, and they immediately befriended him. They invited him to their apartment for a meal and he expressed his surprise that Christians would invite him in knowing he had been with ISIS. He asked why they were so willing to do this.

"This question opened up an immediate door to sharing the Gospel. It was not long before the friendship established by these two men led Omar to commit his life to Christ.

"Vernon and I met him soon after he came to Christ. We sat on the street talking with him and had to move numerous times because ISIS soldiers were following him. Their goal was to take him back to Mosul to face extreme persecution.

"Omar had a gruesome assignment during his time with ISIS. While group executions are a common occurrence wherever ISIS has control, it was Omar's responsibility to make certain everyone being executed was actually dead. If they weren't, he would fire the killing shot into their heads.

"He still wakes up from nightmares, reliving what he has done, but God's grace is sustaining him.

"During those days, his desire for learning the Bible was insatiable. Even knowing that ISIS has a price on his head has not discouraged him from learning what it means to be a leader. He told our Iraqi partner that someday he wants to be a leader and church planter just like him.

"As a refugee, he is also a leader in planting churches among persecuted believers and has personally started many house churches.

"He truly is a modern-day Apostle Paul."

HOW YOU CAN PRAY

Pray for healing and restoration for refugees who lost everything and still have no permanent home.

Pray for peace as millions of innocent people have been directly affected by violence and hatred.

The lack of legal punishment for criminals in Iraq who commit honor crimes contributes to the increase of violence and murders against women and children. Pray for an end to these honor crimes.

TEN

SYRIA

Trying to Heal

2021 WORLD WATCH LIST

Rank: #12
Persecution type: Islamic oppression
Religion: Islam
Persecution level: Extreme
Population: 18,924,000
Christian: 677,000
Government: Presidential Republic

Source: Open Doors

SYRIA

In his kindness God called you to share in his eternal glory by means of Christ Jesus. So after you have suffered a little while, he will restore, support, and strengthen you, and he will place you on a firm foundation.   — 1 PETER 5:10

T he terror comes to Amani in flashes. She remembers rockets shrieking overhead as her family fled their home in Syria. She can still hear the bellowing booms of shells exploding and destroying the homes and buildings in her old neighborhood.

Even eight years later, the image of radicals shoving one of her neighbors into a barrel and lighting him on fire — all while the man screamed for help — is burned into her 14-year-old mind.

But the thing Amani remembers most is the overwhelming fear that consumed her. Her family ran as fast as they could to escape and decided to split up to increase their chances. One half headed for the mountains, and the other ran toward the valley.

Amani's heart raced as she ran, frantically trying to keep up with her parents. She was only 6 at the time, so she doesn't remember much else — just that she feels more at ease in their new home close to the Syrian border ... even though they live in a refugee camp.

In addition to the challenges of refugee life, Amani's family has struggled even more since her father died. As the oldest daughter, Amani does her best to help her mother. She pitches in with chores, looks after her younger siblings, and tries to set an example for them at school.

Her favorite subjects are history and geography, and her dream is to one day be a doctor so she can provide for her family.

Despite the trauma of her past, Amani is doing well in her classes. Her teacher even acknowledges that she'll be an amazing doctor if she can continue her education.

But first, she needs to heal from her emotional scars.

A COUNTRY IN CRISIS

The Syrian Civil War, which began in March 2011, ignited when protesters demanded an end to the authoritarian practices of the government — which, in turn, used violence to suppress demonstrations.

As the conflict escalated, millions of Syrians were displaced from their homes, fearful of the destruction and death they were being forced to face every day.

While many of those fleeing their homes found temporary safety in other parts of Syria, many more fled to neighboring countries, settling in refugee camps that sprang up throughout the region.

Most of these camps were overcrowded with extended families often living together in tents that were suffocating in the summer and freezing in the winter. Food, hygiene supplies, and clean water were always in short supply.

Syria was once known for religious tolerance. However, in more recent years, Syrian Christians have faced opposition common in the region's more restricted Islamist nations. Christians often suffer the loss of jobs, homes, social standing, and family relationships. Christians who share the Gospel face opposition from both extremists and the government.

Thousands have been forced from their homes by the threat of Islamic rebels and jihadist militants. In some areas, Christians have been ordered to convert to Islam, pay a religious tax, or face death.

Christian women have been the targets of sexual violence. Hundreds of Christians are feared to have been kidnapped by terrorists.

Another form of persecution has affected nearly all the Christian families. They are not allowed to teach their children about Christianity, even in private schools. School textbooks have also been found to teach hatred and intolerance toward non-Muslims.

Not surprisingly, mob violence against Christians frequently goes unpunished.

"WE HAVE TO GO!"

She had lost count of how many times she'd looked around the room to check and make sure all her children were safe.

Nada and her husband, Jameel, had opened their home to extended family members who lost their own homes during the Syrian Civil War. But as the fighting drew closer to their village, the couple — along with their oldest son, Evaan; twin girls, Sarina and Martina; and 7-month-old, Roland, gathered with everyone in the front room ... and waited.

When Nada and Jameel first heard the rumors that the fighting was moving their way, they debated every night whether it was time to leave.

"When Roland is a little bit older, the journey will be easier," Nada told Jameel. But by the time the civil war arrived in their area, it was too late to escape.

Now, Nada sat silently and wondered how different things might have been if they had left when they had the chance.

Just then, the house ripped in two. A barrel bomb packed with explosives crashed through the roof, destroying everything in its path.

Nada looked down to see herself covered in blood — but she was unsure whose it was. "We have to go!" Jameel shouted as he scooped up the twins, grabbed their travel bag, and pulled Nada toward what was left of their doorway.

Nada nearly collapsed as they went past the place where Evaan had been standing moments ago. Now there was just a pile of rubble — with a dark, red stain forming underneath. With a final glance around, all Jameel and Nada saw were the mangled bodies of family members. The five of them — Jameel, Nada, the twins, and baby Roland — were the only survivors.

They escaped to the countryside, but the war followed them there. Soon, there was no food left to buy, and Roland's tiny body started wasting away.

Several months later, the siege was broken, and the family lined up with thousands of others at the evacuation point. After five hours of waiting, they were loaded onto a crowded bus.

But when they arrived at their stop, Nada expected to see a crowd — but only a few families milled around. Jameel asked an elderly man what was going on.

"Didn't you hear?" he said. "The convoy of other buses was stopped by militants. They killed most of the men and kidnapped the women and children."

There are approximately **677,000** Christians in Syria, about 3.6 percent of a population of almost 19 million. The ongoing civil war has made the country a breeding ground for Christian persecution.

Source: Open Doors

Nada and Jameel were horrified. They knew they must leave Syria if they wanted to keep their family safe.

They had overheard some people saying if you could make it through Turkey, then you could pay for passage across the sea — where you would be safe.

After many days of exhausting travel by foot, Jameel

and Nada made it to the border of Turkey. The next day, the family walked to a run-down house where they had been told a smuggler would make them a deal. He told them he could get them on a boat to Greece for $1,000 a piece.

When they meet him a couple days later, the "boat" turned out to be a tiny dinghy made for no more than 30 people — instead of the 50 he had assigned to each boat.

Less than four miles from the Turkish shore, the boat began to deflate, and people started to panic. Several men, including Jameel, jumped overboard to lighten the load, and the small boat headed back to where it came from.

Jameel went looking for the smuggler the next morning, who refused to give him his money back but told him he could get the family on a bigger boat — for $3,000 a person.

That wiped out the couple's finances, but they didn't feel like they had much choice. They were hopeful they could quickly find jobs once they got to Greece.

When they arrived to get onboard later that week, they found this "boat" was no bigger than the first one — but contained 60 people now instead of the 30 it was supposed to hold.

Once again, the boat got within sight of the Greek shoreline when Nada began to feel water slosh against her foot. The bottom of the boat was filling with water ... again.

To lighten the load, passengers began throwing items overboard. Someone snatched Nada's bag off her lap — which contained their documentation papers — and threw it into the sea.

Nada froze, not knowing what to do. Without those

papers, it would be nearly impossible to get asylum or apply for jobs in Europe.

The family finally made it to Greece, but Nada couldn't hold back the tears any longer. She had lost so much ... and now she had lost hope.

"I'm so sorry," Jameel whispered to her as he also began to weep. Then he fell to the ground and clung to his children.

Now, I must tell you this is not just one true story.

It's a compilation of several true stories — some about Christians I've personally met, and some I've heard from our partners on the ground. They all have faced severe persecution.

I can see many of their faces in my mind. I can remember their names. I wish you could see them yourselves and hear their stories from their own lips.

That's why I wanted to share this story with you because I'm afraid it's too easy for us to see something on the news about persecution and to quicky move on. But there is no moving on for these men, women, and children. They have suffered greatly for their faith.

GOOD COMES OUT OF TRAGEDY

It was in the Syrian refugee camps where I met Amira and heard her tragic story. Amira and her family had lived near Daraa. As a 14-year-old, Amira loved helping her mother in the kitchen.

But one day, while working beside her mother preparing dinner, tragedy struck. A bomb exploded right next to her home, shaking the entire house. A large kettle of boiling oil on the stove flew into the air, the entire contents splashing across Amira's body.

Amira screamed in pain as the scalding oil blistered across her back, arms, and legs. During the bombardment, her parents rushed her to the hospital where all they could do was try to ease her pain. A lack of supplies made it impossible to do anything about the inevitable scarring that would result from the third-degree burns.

Too frightened to remain in Syria, the family quickly packed up as many belongings as they could fit in a few suitcases and fled to Jordan.

A Christian worker at a free medical clinic provided by World Help in Jordan introduced me to Amira. Tears came to my eyes as she described that horrible day. I thought, "What if that had been one of my daughters?"

Amira showed me photos of the terrible scars that marked her body. It would take $10,000 for surgeries to remove scar tissue, restore movement, and eliminate the pain she was having — funds her family simply did not have. What could I do?

An American family generously provided for Amira's surgeries. I was overjoyed that she would receive help. For the first time since I'd met Amira, a soft smile touched her face when we told her that she could begin the long process of healing.

The impact on Amira's life went far beyond helping heal her physical and emotional wounds. Her entire family was Muslim.

As Amira experienced the love and care she needed

during the worst situation she had ever faced, her heart was softened to the message of the Gospel, and she soon became a Christ-follower. Before long, most members of her family also became believers.

And the story continues. Having gone through such a traumatic experience as a young teenager, she wanted to help others who had faced similar situations. She started volunteering at that medical clinic in Jordan, including visiting several small refugee camps near the border that were home to Syrians from the same area of the country where she used to live.

She talks with children and teens who have faced more hardships than anyone their ages should ever have to face. She shares her story, the struggles and fears she experienced, and the hope and encouragement she received from loving Christian workers at the medical clinic.

She has been able to comfort and encourage so many because she has been able to face her fears and receive physical, emotional, and spiritual healing. Good can come out of the worst situations in life.

Amira determined to develop her skills so that she could work more effectively at the medical clinic where she is now serving full time, enrolling in a technical school to study computer and English. And because of her story and her positive outlook on life, she was given a full scholarship.

LIVING AMONG STRANGERS

Salaam, the owner of a clothing factory, and his family are from Aleppo. Most of his family fled to America when the fighting began. But Salaam decided to move his family to a nearby town and wait out the fighting.

Although ISIS has mostly been driven out of Syria, Christians still live in constant danger because of Islamic extremist groups.

More than **6.6 million** Syrians have fled the country to escape violence since 2011.

Source: U.N. Refugee Agency

A short time later, the militants arrived at his home and forced Salaam and his wife to stand in their yard while each was stripped naked and mercilessly interrogated.

After the soldiers left, the couple fled their home immediately and hid for hours in an abandoned building. Knowing that the soldiers would return, Salaam sent his wife, daughter, and mother to a relative's house where they hid for over two weeks while he prepared for them to leave Syria.

On the way to visit his family, he was kidnapped, beaten, and kept blindfolded in a building for four days.

Leaving everything behind, Salaam and his family were finally able to cross the border into Jordan, where they now live in a crowded, disease-ridden building with dozens of strangers.

I can't even begin to imagine. Leaving everything you know ... your extended family, your clothes, your furniture, your home ... uprooting your life and family to go somewhere you've never been, surrounded by people you don't even know.

WALKING BY FAITH

Crouching behind a crumbling stone structure, 11-year-old Habib peered out into the dusty, debris-ridden street. He tiptoed wearily around piles of rubble and broken glass and around the stiff bodies of men, women, and children sprawled in the streets. It was nearing dusk and the temperature was dropping steadily.

"It's clear. We can go now," Habib whispered to his mother who had been waiting with his two younger sisters behind the charred remnants of an old truck. Even in the twilight, he could see her eyes flicker with relief as she saw his face.

Habib's family had been hiding in Syria for nearly three years. Shelling had destroyed everything around them,

Over and over they asked, "Do you call yourself a Christian?" Each time, his father, bleeding profusely, answered "Yes."

including his father's business. Most of Habib's friends had left a long time ago, disappearing silently in the night. He had seen others gunned down in the street, their pleas for mercy still echoing endlessly in his mind.

After hearing about the conditions in the refugee camps along the Syrian border, the family had remained in their war-torn village, hoping for a swift resolution and a return to peace. But peace never came.

Then, their family home was invaded and ransacked by militants. They mercilessly beat Habib's father and brutally harassed his mother. Over and over they asked, "Do you call yourself a Christian?" Each time, his father, bleeding profusely, answered "Yes."

The last time Habib saw his father, he was being dragged away to be executed in the street. A neighbor, who witnessed the horror unfolding, ran to help Habib and his mother and siblings escape while the fighters were outside. After many days of running, they were exhausted, starving, and terrified.

One evening, the neighbor went out to search for food; he never came back. It was now up to Habib to lead his family to safety. Flashes of light from exploding shells boomed in the distance but seemed to be getting closer. They ran.

The lights of the border crossing into Jordan were just ahead. Leaving behind his home, his identity, and his father ... he gripped his mother's and sister's hands and stepped forward into the night.

THE LITTLEST VICTIM

Mara has been living in a refugee camp on the Syrian border for more than eight years now, but before the war, she was a farmer. Mara lived close to her extended family. Together, they raised goats, cows, and sheep.

Her life was good, and she was happy.

"We suffer a lot, and we're used to that. But without medications for the children, it's just too much."

Then the attacks came. After seeing violent shootings near their home, Mara's family ran for their lives. There was no time to gather supplies. They left with nothing — no food, no money, and no way to make a living.

For a while, the family settled in with one of Mara's cousins. They had just begun to rebuild their lives. Mara was even pregnant again and hopeful for the future — but the violence followed them.

Their home was raided. Mara was separated from much of her family, and in the process, she suffered a miscarriage.

She was heartbroken and had nowhere to go.

Since then, Mara has reunited with much of her family. However, every day is a struggle to survive in the refugee camp. Although she no longer fears daily raids or shootings, she is still afraid.

Two of her six children have developed severe health problems. Her 4-year-old needs surgery to improve her vision and hearing, and her 11-year-old has a serious nervous system disorder. Mara can't afford the medical help they need.

Mara's family has little to call their own. And when I think of the least of these, I think of families like hers. I think of parents waiting in long lines, hoping to get just a little bit of food for their starving children. I think of precious little kids, suffering from injuries that could be easily treated.

I'll never forget the smiles on the faces of children I met as I handed them a brightly colored winter hat before I left the camp.

When you've lost everything, even the smallest gifts are a source of hope.

SHE RECEIVED MORE THAN MEDICINE

While visiting Syrian refugees, I also met a woman who had become a Christ-follower because someone had shown her the love of Jesus when she needed it most.

Sabeen has been through so much. When violence broke out in Syria, her 11-year-old daughter was almost raped, and her 8-year-old son was nearly kidnapped. She couldn't sleep at night because she was so afraid. Her family fled, but they were captured and held prisoner with little food or water for 21 days.

Finally, after so much suffering, Sabeen arrived in a refugee camp and learned about our free clinic run by Christian doctors. She went there looking for medical help

— but she found so much more.

The doctors were so compassionate she couldn't help but ask them why. After all, she was a Muslim. They were Christians. Why would they care about her?

They told her about Jesus' love and how He commanded us to love others. She soon surrendered to that love. Sabeen and her entire family became Christ followers.

HOW YOU CAN PRAY

Pray for physical and spiritual healing and restoration for refugees who lost everything and continue to live in difficult circumstances.

Pray for the safety and wellness of Syria's children. Because of the country's health system deterioration, many have not been immunized or kept current on vaccinations. Due to chaotic and crowded conditions, children are also more vulnerable to sexual abuse and exploitation.

Pray for stability throughout the Middle East and the millions of innocent people who have been affected directly by violence and hatred.

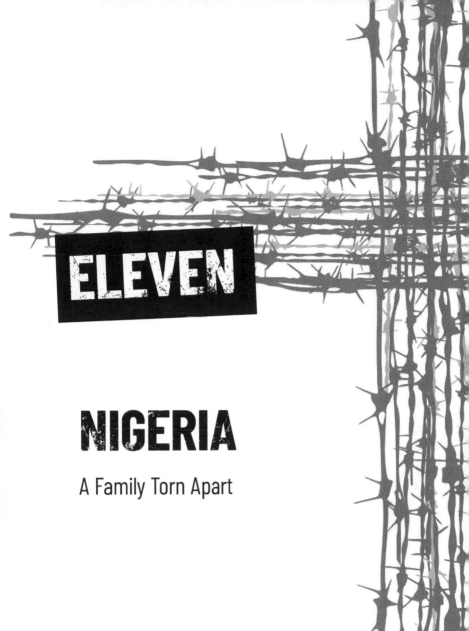

ELEVEN

NIGERIA

A Family Torn Apart

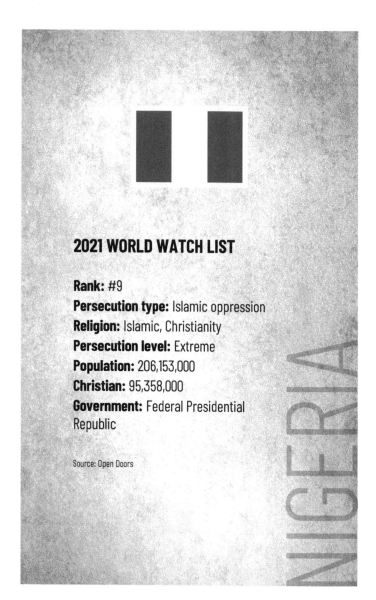

2021 WORLD WATCH LIST

Rank: #9
Persecution type: Islamic oppression
Religion: Islamic, Christianity
Persecution level: Extreme
Population: 206,153,000
Christian: 95,358,000
Government: Federal Presidential Republic

Source: Open Doors

If one part suffers, all the parts suffer with it, and if one part is honored, all the parts are glad.   — 1 CORINTHIANS 12:26

A bednego, 15, and his siblings crawled into bed after a long day of working in the fields. They knew they needed to be rested for school the next morning.

But their eyes had just closed when they heard the shots. It was the Fulani herdsman, a nomadic group who has been terrorizing villages across Nigeria.

Abednego jumped out of bed, then froze. Several large men had forced their way into the house. They demanded money, took what they could find, and then turned their machetes on the children.

In seconds, two of his siblings were dead and another unconscious. His youngest sister, Goodness, clutched her bleeding face. And Abednego himself struggled to stand on a broken leg. His young body is now covered with scars — scars that will never go away.

"I just want to go home," Abednego says quietly, as he sits with Goodness in a refugee camp.

"CONVERT OR BE KILLED"

One of our partners in Nigeria recently asked us to pray specifically for the northeast part of the country, saying, "Boko Haram has almost succeeded in uprooting the Christian community in northeastern Nigeria. It is very clear that their intention is to Islamize Nigeria.

"Honest people will be sleeping in their homes at night, and in the morning, what you will see are dead bodies." A loose English definition of Boko Haram is "Western ways are forbidden."

Boko Haram and the Fulani herdsmen, two militant Islamic groups, continue to terrorize Christians and have forced millions to flee their homes.

More than **2,200** Christians were killed in Nigeria during 2020 at the hands of radical Islamists.

Source: Open Doors

Another Nigerian pastor added, "Pray for Christians in Nigeria especially in the north, who are going through severe persecution for their faith. Many of them have lost most of their belongings to these insurgents and are depending on the help they receive from the Christian body to survive."

These earnest requests reminded me of a story I heard several months ago about a young Nigerian woman I'll call Esther.

When Boko Haram militants attacked her village, Esther and her children ran for safety. She hid her children in the village's graveyard beneath grass and leaves, and told them to be quiet. She hid behind the door of a makeshift outhouse.

The terrorists shouted, "Convert or be killed!" as they systematically went through the village terrorizing people. Hoping she wouldn't be discovered, Esther held her breath as the radicals drew closer.

The massacre lasted five hours.

Esther watched in horror as the men set fire to her neighbors' occupied homes and then set fire to her church. The young mother placed a protective hand on her growing belly.

Finally, when the rampage was over, she gathered her children and ran to her father's house.

She said a quick prayer before heading through the door.

Her sister-in-law's body, riddled with bullet holes, was lying on the floor — her intestines spilled out of her body.

As Esther struggled to comprehend the horror before her, searing pain wracked her body. She doubled over, clutching her stomach.

Boko Haram had taken another victim — the life of her unborn child.

NOTHING SHORT OF A MIRACLE

If you question whether God is still in the miracle business, then just ask Gail if she believes.

She was attacked not once, not twice ... but four times by Boko Haram, the deadly Islamic terrorist group in

Nigeria. And God miraculously saved her life each time.

Gail and her family were sitting in church one Sunday morning when suddenly something crashed through the window and onto the floor. It took a moment before anyone realized what it was.

"A bomb!" someone shouted.

Everyone ducked for cover and braced for the blast — but it never came.

The bomb that Boko Haram soldiers had hurled through the window, hoping to wipe out an entire congregation of Christians, was defective.

But the soldiers weren't going to give up that easily. They waited until dark and attacked. They burned houses, churches, and schools.

"It was a nightmare," Gail recalls.

Gail, her mother, and her younger siblings were all kidnapped and taken deep into the forest.

Gail attempted to escape but was caught. One of the militants slashed a razor blade across her Achilles tendon. As she screamed, the soldier screamed right back in her face.

"Try to escape again, and we will kill you!"

Undeterred, she and her mother began planning their next escape attempt. They waited until the soldiers were distracted one night and then silently shimmied up the nearest tree.

When the soldiers returned to find the family gone, they were furious and began shooting blindly into the trees, hoping to hit the runaways.

"God please protect us," the family prayed. And He did. God directed that wild spray of bullets so not even one came close to them.

"Try to escape again, and we will kill you!"

Finally, the soldiers moved on, and Gail's family was able to climb down and escape. They went to Gail's grandfather's house where they hoped they would be safe.

But Boko Haram found them there, too. The terrorists burst into the house and demanded that Gail's grandfather convert to Islam or die.

"I will not deny Christ," he declared. He even began preaching to the terrorists while they attacked him.

Gail begged them to stop. In response, they knocked her to the ground and executed her grandfather right in front of her.

Next, they lunged at Gail to kidnap her, but God gave her the strength to escape. A young girl like her shouldn't have been able to outrun an entire group of armed men — but she did.

Not long after reuniting with the rest of her family, Gail and her younger sister were alone one day when they were attacked again by Boko Haram terrorists. The terrorists had already captured many other people as well, some of them Christians and some of them Muslims.

They announced to the Muslim captives that they would begin killing the Christians in front of them as a warning of what happens to people who turn from Islam.

One of the soldiers pointed his gun at the first Christian. Gail could hardly watch as the man pulled the trigger. She steeled herself for the gunshot, for the screams. She prayed for God to deliver them. She waited … but all she heard was a soft *click.*

The gun wouldn't fire.

The man pointed his gun at another Christian. Click! Nothing happened.

One of the others tried his gun. Nothing. A third terrorist pulled his trigger. Still nothing.

Finally, the terrorists decided to "test" their guns on the Muslim prisoners. The guns fired perfectly, and the Muslim prisoners fell to the ground. The kidnappers, callous to the fact that they had just shot their own people, turned back to the Christians.

They fired … but again, *nothing happened.*

The militants were so confused and amazed by the miracle they were witnessing that they let Gail and the rest of the Christians go.

FROM PERSECUTOR TO BELIEVER

My wife, Patty, and I always tried to make sure our children grew up in a Christian home. If the church doors were open, our family was sitting in one of the pews.

Unfortunately, people like Jina don't have that kind of home life. Jina was born into a Muslim family in Nigeria who hated Christians, so you can imagine how angry they were when Jina became a believer.

Jina was just like the rest of her family at one time. They wanted churches destroyed and did everything they could to persecute Christians.

But one day Jina was given a copy of God's Word, and her life changed forever. She became a believer!

She stopped hating Christians and started reading the Bible. Her family noticed the transformation in Jina's life, and they didn't like it. One of her older brothers became so angry that he beat her and threw her belongings out of the house.

It was around this time that Boko Haram terrorists invaded Jina's village. They killed anyone they found and burned almost every house to the ground.

Jina and one of her sisters were separated from the rest of the family. Thankfully, a rescue vehicle arrived and drove Jina and her sister to a displacement camp.

Jina was grateful to be alive.

Her family had practically disowned her. She had just barely escaped death. Her life was shattered after the terrorist attack.

But she found comfort by reading God's Word.

ACT OF KINDNESS CHANGED HIS LIFE

"I can't go back to Islam."

Those words could have been Hamid's death sentence. He has faced intense persecution in Nigeria since accepting Christ.

Hamid watched the anger fill his father's face after telling him he had renounced the Muslim faith. "I can't go back to Islam," he said. In a fit of rage, Hamid's father grabbed an ax and swung.

That's when Hamid fled for his life. He ran from village to village, but his father ordered Hamid's brothers and other Muslim teenagers to chase after him. It didn't matter that Hamid was his own flesh and blood.

He wanted him dead.

Like Hamid, many believers in places like Nigeria, China, North Korea, and Iran are facing the threat of abuse, imprisonment, and even death because of their faith.

Hamid grew up as a devout Muslim. He was his father's favorite because he also hated Christianity. As a young adult, he often burned churches and attacked believers in their homes during religious ceremonies.

"He was [very] popular in agitating a riot."

But one act of kindness changed the course of Hamid's life forever.

As Hamid was planning his next attack, a Christian elder stepped outside and approached him. The gentleman carried something in his arms. Instead of preaching or trying to change Hamid's mind, the elder held out his hands and offered Hamid some new clothes.

"With all the havoc I caused the Christian families, they were still kind to me," Hamid said.

Hamid tossed and turned that night. For days he couldn't forget about the man's generosity. Unable to stand it any longer, Hamid ran to a nearby church, spoke to the pastor — and gave his life to Christ.

Hamid escaped his father's reach for several years. He settled in a small village where a Christian elder provided him with shelter and Bible training. Eventually, he started a business where he would travel in his truck and sell meat to customers.

> **More Christians are murdered for their faith in Nigeria than in any other country.**
>
> Source: Open Doors

Hamid was enjoying his new life — but his father found him again.

He devised a plan for some other Muslim youths to ambush Hamid's car. They tampered with the wires and brakes causing Hamid to have an accident. He hit another vehicle, and the driver was killed. Hamid's father quickly reported his son to Islamic authorities, and he was thrown into prison without a fair trial.

"I was extremely tortured for 22 days in the prison," Hamid said. "I almost lost my memory because of the pains, but I refused to deny Christ. I still told my father that I would never go back to Islam."

Even in the midst of persecution, Hamid's faith didn't waver.

Christian elders found out about Hamid's dilemma and had some respectable lawyers rescue him. Sore and scarred from his beatings, Hamid returned to his village. He continued his business, started farming, and started his own family.

But persecution followed him.

Muslim extremists in the community raided his house and tried to kill him. They took him to court, but Hamid won the case. Other radicals ambushed him on the road, but Hamid dodged the bullets. They even tried to poison him in the market — but God delivered him.

> "... I refused to deny Christ. I still told my father that I would never go back to Islam."

Despite the constant suffering, Hamid continued to secretly minister to other believers in his village. "He became more popular in fighting for the right of Christians," our partner said.

Hamid wasn't just popular with believers. The Islamic militant group Boko Haram had heard of him, as well. And when they saw him driving his truck one day, they stopped him.

As Hamid stepped out of his truck, he found himself face to face with the metal barrels of eight loaded guns.

Hamid held up his hands and silently began praying.

"When I saw them, I was thinking my end has come because they were ready to shoot me," Hamid said. "But God gave me wisdom, and I spoke to them in the Kanuri language."

And that's how God saved Hamid that day on the side of the road under the blistering sun. He switched dialects when he spoke, so the soldiers thought he was a different person. Not the infamous Hamid who was spreading Christianity.

Because of his faith, Hamid walked away unscathed.

God spared Hamid's life repeatedly. Boko Haram attacked his village multiple times, burning houses and slaughtering anyone who stood in their way. And on more than one occasion, Hamid has found himself surrounded by rifles and angry soldiers.

But he's clung to the promises of God's Word each time.[37]

THEIR CRIES FOR HELP

Nigeria continues to rise on Open Doors' World Watch List as persecution has worsened in both public and private life. In the past few years, militants have begun stopping commercial vehicles to remove Christians and either abduct or execute them.

It has become so violent that few schools are open, and parents are concerned about their children's education. Terrorists rape and murder women. They kidnap young children. They burn down houses, schools, and churches.

This horrifying brutality is taking a toll on the vulnerable Christian community, despite their deep faith and devotion.

We must not turn a deaf ear to their cries for help. God has not forgotten or abandoned these precious brothers and sisters ... neither can we.

HOW YOU CAN PRAY

Pray that the persecution of the church will glorify God and lead to the further spread of the Gospel.

Pray for the hundreds of children who have been kidnapped by terrorists.

Pray that church leaders will not be intimidated but will speak boldly for Christ and place an emphasis on discipleship and balanced Bible teaching.

Pray that the Christian community would not lose hope but stand strong in the face of brutal persecution.

EPILOGUE

Thousands of persecuted Christians worldwide are taking the Martyr's Oath. I pray you will stand with your brothers and sisters who have not only taken this oath, but are willing to die if necessary for their faith. If they are willing to die to follow Jesus, surely we can live to follow Jesus. I invite you to take this oath today.

THE MARTYR'S OATH

I AM A FOLLOWER OF JESUS .I believe He lived and walked among us, was crucified for our sins, and was raised from the dead, according to the Scriptures. I believe He is the King of the earth, who will come back for his church.

As He has given His life for me, so I am willing to give my life for Him. I will use every breath I possess to boldly proclaim His gospel. Whether abundance or need, in safety or peril, in peace or distress, I will not – I cannot – keep quiet. His unfailing love is better than life, and His grace compels me to speak His name even if His name costs me everything. Even in the face of death, I will not deny Him. And should shadow and darkness encroach upon me, I will not fear, for I know He is always with me.

Though persecution may come, I know my battle is not against flesh but against the forces of evil. I will not hate those whom God has called me to love.

Therefore, I will forgive when ridiculed, show mercy when struck, and love when hated. I will clothe myself with meekness and kindness so those around me may see the face of Jesus reflected in me, especially if they abuse me.

I have taken up my cross; I have laid everything else down. I know my faith could cost me my life, but I will follow and love Jesus until the end, whenever and however that end may come. Should I die for Jesus, I confess that my death is not to achieve salvation but in gratitude for the grace I've already received. I will not die to earn my reward in heaven, but because Jesus has already given me the ultimate reward in the forgiveness of my sins and the salvation of my soul.

For me to live is Christ: for me to die is gain.[38]

In Jesus name,
Amen

HOW TO GET INVOLVED

Can you imagine never having a Bible of your own … or even holding one? Many people around the world have never had the opportunity to read God's Word for themselves. But when you become a *Bibles for All* **Ambassador,** you help change that.

Bibles for All Ambassadors are people who pledge to give every month to send Bibles to people around the world.

When you commit to a monthly gift of $30, you will send three Bibles each month to people who have never owned one. And since Bibles are shared among family and friends, your gift multiplies. Each copy of God's Word will impact at least five people!

Each month, your gift will provide God's Word to some of the world's largest Bible deserts — places where it is almost impossible to find a copy of the Scriptures. These Bible deserts include countries such as India, where entire communities have never been reached with the Gospel, and nations such as China, where believers face intense persecution for their faith.

Visit worldhelp.net/BiblesForAll to learn more and to give.

Want to help persecuted believers and people in need around the world? Go to **worldhelp.net/persecuted** or scan the QR code here to help provide items like food, clean water, Bibles, and more.

ACKNOWLEDGMENTS

Howard Erickson
Ryan Feister
Sheryl Martin Hash
Cara Holcomb
Carmen McCauley
Joy Thompson

I'm so grateful for the incredible team that worked with me in editing this book. You are amazing!

ENDNOTES

1. Stoyan Zaimov, "Every 5 minutes a Christian Is martyred for their Faith," https://www.christianpost.com/news/every-5-minutes-a-christian-is-martyred-for-their-faith-persecution-watchdog-group-warns.html, September 16, 2015

2. Samuel Smith, *Over 900,000 Christians Martyred for their Faith in Last 10 Years,* Christianpost.com, (Jan 17, 2017)

3. Paul Marshall, *Their Blood Cries Out,* (Dallas: World Publishing, 1997): 151: back cover

4. *Fox's Book of Martyrs*

5. Jeff Taylor, "Persecution Today," *World Christian,* (September 1999): 16

6. Mark Batterson, *Play the Man,* (Michigan: Baker Publishing Group, 2017) 7-8

7. Open Doors, "World Watch List 2020: Trends," https://www.opendoorsuk.org/persecution/wwl20-trends/

8. David Stravers, former executive, Bible League

9. Paul Marshall, *Their Blood Cries Out,* (Dallas: World Publishing, 1997): 151; letter dated August 2, 1995

10. *Fox's Book of Martyrs*

11. Open Doors, https://www.opendoorsuk.org/persecution/wwl20-trends/

12. "Christian persecution at near genocide levels," BBC News, https://www.bbc.com/news/uk-48146305. May 3, 2019. Quote by the Right Rev. Philip Mounstephen, Bishop of Truro

13. Mark Galli, "Sometimes Persecution Purifies, Unifies and Grows

the Church," Christianity Today, (May 19, 1997): 16

14. *Stephen, the Man God Crowned:* 94

15. John Piper, *Let the Nations be Glad:* 91

16. The Martyr's Oath, Tyndale House, 2017, page 12

17. "Religion in China," Council on Foreign Relations. Web. 25 Sept. 2020 https://www.cfr.org/backgrounder/religion-china

18. Matthew 16:18, KJV

19. Vernon Brewer, *Defining Moments* excerpt, updated 2016: 80

20. "Do You Believe in God," The Voice of the Martyrs Special Issue (2002): 12

21. Letter taken from, *The Resurrection of the Chinese Church,* by Tony Lambert: 172-173 and *Heartcry for China,* by Ross Patterson: 191-192

22. Ye Jiajia, "CCP officials: Christianity Doesn't Belong in China," *Bitter Winter* https://bitterwinter.org/ccp-officials-christi-anity-doesnt-belong-in-china/ Oct. 6, 2020

23. David G. Hunt, *The Heavenly Man,* (Canada: World Serve Ministries, 1999): 26-27, 29-30

24. "China Destroys 3,000-Seat Church, Detains Pastors," Christian Post. Web. 21 Oct. 2019 https://www.christianpost.com/news/china-destroys-3000-seat-church-detains-pastors.html?fbclid=IwAR0M

25. "China Turns Churches into Factories, 'Cultural Centers' to Ensure Christians Can't Meet," Christian Post. Web. 10 Nov. 2020 https://www.christianpost.com/news/china-turns-church-es-into-factories-cultural-centers.html?fbclid=IwAR2b-kVolD66zge_MrgH1NYF9i6iP8VtESZvhe8BdFvwBxT-CgyCSDP9GpE8

26. Vernon Brewer, *Defining Moments* excerpt, updated 2016: 112

27. "Light the Window," edited by Floyd McClung

28. "The Devil is Desperate," *The Voice of the Martyrs* Special Issue (2002): 8

29. Open Doors, "World Watch List 2020: Trends," https://www.opendoorsuk.org/persecution/wwl20-trends/

30. Lawrence Elliott, Reader's Digest, September, 1991, 73-78

31. The Jesus Film Project, https://www.jesusfilm.org

32. U.S. Center for World Missions, http://www.uscwm.org/

33. Matthew 11:28

34. John 11:26

35. Adoniram Judson, https://www.wholesomewords.org/missions/bjudson20.html

36. "Christian Leader: ISIS Beheading Children." CNN. Cable News Network, n.d. Web. 10 Nov. 2014 http://www.cnn.com/video/data/2.0/video/world/2014/08/06/idesk-iraq-christians-persecuted-mark-arabo-intv.cnn.html

37. One of our team members recently shared this moving story from one of our partners on the ground in Nigeria.

38. The Martyr's Oath, Tyndale House, 2017

ABOUT THE AUTHOR

VERNON BREWER is the founder of World Help, a Christian humanitarian organization serving the physical and spiritual needs of people in impoverished communities around the world. World Help gives help for today and hope for tomorrow through humanitarian aid, education and sustainability projects, and spiritual development programs such as Bible distribution and church planting.

Vernon has led more than 500 church evangelistic crusades and rallies and has lectured on more than 30 college and university campuses. He has spoken to more than 1 million teenagers in public high school assembly programs and is a frequent conference speaker. He also has preached and led conferences in more than 67 countries worldwide. In addition, he has personally taken over 4,000 people to the mission field.

Vernon's considered to be an outspoken advocate for the persecuted church. He has appeared on various major media outlets, including Fox News, Fox News Radio, and CBN News, to speak about the topic.

Vernon was the first graduate of Liberty University in 1973. He served as Dean of Students and Vice President of Student Development at Liberty University from 1980 –

1992. In 2009, he was named Liberty University Alumnus of the Year. He received an honorary Doctor of Humanities degree from Liberty University in May 2010. In 2015, Vernon was inducted into his public high school's hall of fame. He also is the author of five other books: *The Forgotten Children, Children of Hope, Defining Moments, causelife,* and *Why.*

Vernon and his wife, Patty, have three married daughters, Noel, Nikki, and Jenny; one married son, Josh, and eight grandchildren. Vernon and Patty reside in Forest, Virginia.

ABOUT WORLD HELP

World Help is a Christian humanitarian organization committed to serving the physical and spiritual needs of people in impoverished communities around the world. Since its inception in 1991, World Help has impacted more than 84 million people in 71 countries through humanitarian aid and relief, community development projects, Bible distribution and church planting, child sponsorship, and more.

Learn more at **worldhelp.net.**